IN THE CLAP SHACK

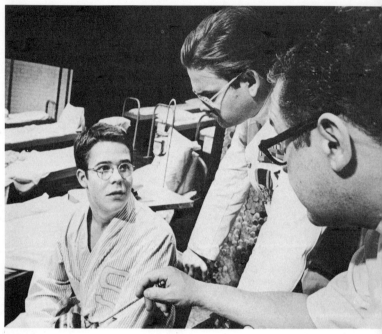

Miles Chapin as MAGRUDER, Paul Schierhorn
as CAPTAIN BUDWINKLE and Jeremy Geidt as
DR. GLANZ.

In The Clap Shack

by WILLIAM STYRON

RANDOM HOUSE / NEW YORK

Photographs by William Baker, courtesy of Yale Repertory Theatre.

Library of Congress Cataloging in Publication Data

Styron, William, 1925–
In the clap shack.

A play.
I. Title.
PS3569.T9I5   812'.5'4   72–11412
ISBN 0–394–46093–6

Manufactured in the United States of America

76-2553

To Robert D. Loomis

IN THE CLAP SHACK *was first presented on December 15, 1972, at the Yale Repertory Theatre in New Haven, Connecticut, with the following cast:*

WALLACE MAGRUDER, *a hospital patient*	Miles Chapin
SCHWARTZ, *a patient*	Eugene Troobnick
DR. GLANZ, *a urologist*	Jeremy Geidt
LINEWEAVER, *pharmacist's mate first-class*	Nicholas Hormann
CAPTAIN BUDWINKLE, *hospital commandant*	Paul Schierhorn
LORENZO CLARK, *a patient*	Hannibal Penney, Jr.
STANCIK, *a patient*	Joseph G. Grifasi
DADARIO, *a patient*	Michael Gross
MCDANIEL, *a patient*	William Ludel
CHALKLEY, *a patient*	Steven Robman
CATHOLIC CHAPLAIN	Bill Gearhart
CHAPLAIN'S ASSISTANT	Thomas E. Lanter
MARINE CORPORAL, *a military policeman*	Steven Robman

THE SCENE

The entire action takes place on the Urological Ward of the
United States Naval Hospital at a large Marine Corps base
in the South. The time is the summer of 1943.

ACT ONE

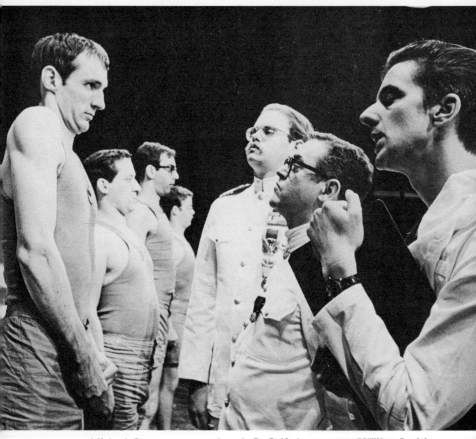

Michael Gross as DADARIO, Joseph G. Grifasi as STANCIK, William Ludel as MC DANIEL, Miles Chapin as MAGRUDER, Paul Schierhorn as CAPTAIN BUDWINKLE, Jeremy Geidt as DR. GLANZ and Nicholas Hormann as LINEWEAVER.

The time is the summer of 1943. The place is the Urological Ward of the United States Naval Hospital at a large Marine Corps base in the South. The entire action of the play takes place on this ward, which differs little in appearance from hospital wards throughout the world. Two rows of about nine beds each, their feet facing each other upon a central aisle, dominate the scene. The beds are staggered, so that the audience obtains a view of each bed and its patient. At extreme stage left is the office of the Chief Urologist, DR. GLANZ, *who rules the ward from this cluttered room filled with urological instruments and medical books. To the right of this office, outside the door and at the end of the ward proper, are the chair and desk occupied by Pharmacist's Mate First-Class* LINEWEAVER, GLANZ*'s satrap and the chief male nurse of the ward.*

Overture: "There's a Star-Spangled Banner Waving Somewhere."

As the lights go up on the curtainless stage, it is a few moments before 6:30 A.M., the hour for reveille, and the occupants of the ward are still asleep. Some stir restlessly in their beds. Others snore. One voice is heard to mumble at intervals a small anguished "Pearl! Pearl!" as if in semidelirium. At his desk, LINEWEAVER, *an effeminate, thin, angular sailor in summer whites, sits making out reports with a pencil. Suddenly he looks at his watch and rises, walking slowly down the aisle as he rouses the men. His air is casual, jaunty; the effeminacy should be quite evident but not over-emphasized or caricatured.*

LINEWEAVER *(His voice an amiable singsong)*   All right, up and at 'em! Rise and shine, you gyrenes! Drop your cocks and grab your socks! VD patients: short-arm inspection in *precisely ten minutes!*

> *(There are groans from the patients as they rouse themselves. Some sit on the edge of their beds and drowsily regard their feet. Others only prop themselves up against their pillows. One or two manage to stand and stretch, clad like the others in green Marine Corps issue underwear. Only a drowsing Negro—obviously quite sick—and the marine who was heard to mutter "Pearl! Pearl!" remain virtually motionless under their sheets, oblivious to* LINEWEAVER'*s verbal assault. One marine, however,* CORPORAL STANCIK, *rolls over as if to remain resolutely asleep and mumbles his resentment to* LINEWEAVER*)*

STANCIK *(His accent is urban, working-class Northeast)* Up yours, Lineweaver, you creep.

LINEWEAVER *(Good-humoredly)* On your feet, Stancik. Dr. Glanz is going to take a look at your tool.

STANCIK Just let me sleep, you faggot.

LINEWEAVER *(Raps the bed with his hand)* I'm not bullshittin' you this morning, Stancik. Dr. Glanz is going to have the Old Man with him. Captain Budwinkle. And you guys have got to look *very* superior.

> (STANCIK *stirs awake as* DADARIO, *a patient standing nearby flexing his muscles and yawning, responds with drowsy sarcasm)*

DADARIO How can a dozen guys look superior at six-thirty in the morning all lined up with their peckers hanging out?

LINEWEAVER *(Keeping his good humor)* Just use a little imagination, Dadario. *(In a semi-aside)* I think you *all* look *cute.*

STANCIK *(Now climbing out of bed)* You would. *(Yawns)* Boy, did I have a dirty dream.

LINEWEAVER Like I say, Stancik, I think you've got an obsession. It's dreams like that that get you into this joint in the first place.
(He pauses at the bedside of the patient who had been calling "Pearl! Pearl!" This is a marine private in his mid-twenties named CHALKLEY. *The sick man is now awake but is flushed and sweating, and he has the glassy, distracted look of one who is very ill and in extreme discomfort.* LINE-WEAVER *takes his pulse and sticks a thermometer in his mouth, then marks something on the chart which is attached to the end of each bed. As he does this, the other patients are frittering the minutes away in various fashions: some leaf through magazines and comic books, a few do desultory setting-up exercises, others resume a three-handed card game, one turns on a portable radio which plays "Don't Fence Me In." Two patients near* CHALKLEY's *bed, in the meantime, are talking about him)*

DADARIO Did you hear Chalkley? Did you hear him, Schwartz? All night long he kept saying "Pearl, Pearl!" It gave me the creeps. I couldn't sleep. Who do you guess that fucking Pearl is?

SCHWARTZ *(A solemn, bespectacled Jew, perhaps a few years older than the other patients, most of whom are in their early twenties. He raises his eyes from a book)* It's his sister. She's the closest relative he's got. She was run down by a car—in Atlanta, I think. She's in very bad shape. Chalkley told me about her last week, before he got so sick. Poor guy.

DADARIO They should put a guy like that off somewhere by himself, in some room, for his own good and ours. I can't stand to hear him say "Pearl, Pearl!" all night. It gives you the creeps.

SCHWARTZ *(Returns to the book)* Poor guy.

STANCIK *(To DADARIO)* Are you an ass man or a tit man, Dadario? Me, I'm an ass man. Someday I'm goin' to find me an ass with a pair of handles. Then I'm goin' to really operate.

DADARIO *(He is shaving himself with an electric shaver)* Frankly, I'm for ass *and* tits, Stancik. A sense of proportion is what's needed in the world, if you ask me.

LINEWEAVER *(Pauses at the bed of the Negro, a Southern-born private named LORENZO CLARK. The Negro is awake but appears to be very feeble)* How do you feel this morning, Lorenzo? All bright-eyed and bushy-tailed?

CLARK Man, I've had better mornin's. Each mornin' 'pears to be a little darker than the last. *(He is speaking very slowly)* How do it feel today?

LINEWEAVER *(Taking his pulse)* Checks out fine, Lorenzo. Steady as she goes. *(There is a note of false jollity in his voice)* You'll be out of here by Labor Day, eatin' barbecued spareribs and humpin' those little jungle bunnies over in Port Royal like a real stud. Feel like you can down a little chow this morning?

CLARK *(Haltingly)* I feels pretty poorly. Guess you'd better let me just rest a bit.

LINEWEAVER Where you headin', gyrene?
(He intercepts a very young marine who is trying politely to press past him. This is a private named WALLY MA- GRUDER. He is dressed in the same kind of white hospital robe that some of the other patients have already donned. One is struck almost immediately by this boy's bewilder-

*ment, his vulnerability, and by his wistfulness and inno-
cence)*

MAGRUDER   I—I have to go to the bathroom. I mean, the
head.

LINEWEAVER *(Emphatically)*   Unh-unh! Not till I check your
diagnosis. You're a new face. Didn't you come in last
night during the other duty watch?

MAGRUDER   Yeah, I came in about ten o'clock. I—

LINEWEAVER *(Inspecting* MAGRUDER*'s chart)*   Ah, "Wallace
Magruder, private, serial number five-four-two-three-oh-
seven, age eighteen, born Danville, Virginia. Expert rifle-
man, graduate 417th recruit platoon. Serological tests reveal syphilis." *Syphilis! (Turns to* MAGRUDER *almost
admiringly)* As I live and breathe, a real live syphilitic!
And a three plus on your Kahn *and* your Wassermann—
almost at the top. Aren't *you* the raunchy devil! An aristo-
crat among the votaries of Venus, heir to the malady of
Casanova, De Maupassant and Baudelaire. Welcome
aboard, Magruder. We haven't had a syphilitic in here
since last month. *(Gestures toward the rest of the patients, a
few of whose attention has been caught by the encounter)* Amid
all of this common, garden-variety gonorrhea your afflic-
tion stands out like poison oak. *(An aside)* I'm joking like
crazy, but I'm crying inside. It's *really* almost incurable.

DADARIO *(To* STANCIK*)*   Now *there* is an ass *and* tit man. See
what I mean?

LINEWEAVER   Among these plain old clapped-up types you
walk as a prince among commoners. But you still can't go
to the head.

MAGRUDER *(With pain in his voice)*   Why can't I go to the
head? It's really—

LINEWEAVER   Short-arm inspection, Wally. Every morning, *sharp* at six-forty, a short-arm inspection by Dr. Glanz. And this morning there'll also be Captain Budwinkle, the new hospital commandant.

MAGRUDER   But I've always thought that a short-arm inspection was just for the clap. I mean—
>   *(At this moment, a light goes up in the office of the Chief Urologist. Seen entering the room are* DR. GLANZ, *in the uniform of a lieutenant commander, and* CAPTAIN BUDWINKLE. DR. GLANZ *is a short, officious-looking man with graying hair and spectacles. His every gesture bespeaks obedience to duty and authority.* CAPTAIN BUDWINKLE *looks like a Hollywood version of a Navy captain—imperious, patrician of carriage, aloof and proud. He is decorated with medals and campaign ribbons that go almost to his shoulder.* DR. GLANZ *picks up a sheaf of papers and they converse in pantomine as* LINEWEAVER *continues)*

LINEWEAVER   Pay attention, dopey. It is true that the amount of the clear mucous substance—known amusingly as gleet—which accumulates at the end of the male organ is an index of the effect of treatment for gonorrhea, not syphilis. But since prodigies like yourself are apt in the course of their exploits to pick up *both* diseases, the short-arm is required for you too—at least for the first few days here. Why you are not permitted to pee-pee beforehand should be obvious.

MAGRUDER *(Despairingly)*   All right. God! All right!
>   *(As* DR. GLANZ *begins to speak to* CAPTAIN BUDWINKLE, *the patients continue their early morning routine. It should be made plain that the conversation between the two officers is out of the patients' earshot)*

GLANZ   We think it's a sign, Captain Budwinkle, of the moral breakdown this war has brought about that we've

seen a truly alarming rise in the incidence of venereal
cases. As the Captain well knows, venereal disease has
always been with us in the Navy and Marine Corps. It's
a major problem. But never before have we, personally,
witnessed such a shocking growth.

BUDWINKLE Well, Dr. Glanz, I appreciate your concern
about the VD crisis. Of course I'm no doctor, but as an
administrator, I'm quite alarmed. Washington is also very
much alarmed. Needless to say, I am not here at this
ungodly hour for beer and skittles. One of my first and
most urgent duties on assuming this command is to get
an accurate bearing on our venereal situation. To get a
clear view from the poop deck, that is, so we can navigate
the rocks and shoals.

GLANZ Well, sir, nothing would be more revealing than a
breakdown of the composition of this one urological
ward. *(Gestures with his hand at a chart)* Of our fifteen
patients only four are here for *non*-venereal reasons.
The most serious is a case of pyelonephritis—chronic,
we're afraid. Should have been nipped at the first physical exam, but wasn't, so now he'll die at government
expense. It's definitely a terminal case, since the patient
has developed galloping hypertension. Our second non-
VD is a simple circumcision. Our third is a kidney cal-
culus. Our fourth and last is suspected renal tuberculosis. Jewish chap. No worry about circumcision *there*, eh,
sir? *(Chuckles)* Well, the rest of our patients are entirely
venereal, practically all gonorrhea. It's a thoroughly cor-
rupt and discouraging scene, as the Captain will shortly
see.

BUDWINKLE Just how well do your gonorrhea cases seem to
be responding to the newer sulfa drugs, Glanz? If they're
doing as poorly as I've heard elsewhere we'd better batten
down all ports and hatches and man the fire stations.

GLANZ Generally speaking, your information is correct, sir, though we've seen great improvement in a few individual cases.

BUDWINKLE I gather that among your venereal patients you have a case of granuloma inguinale. How does it seem to be responding to sulfa?

GLANZ Not at all, so far as we can tell, Captain. This colored boy has a badly ulcerated groin and is severely debilitated. We frankly don't give him much hope. He may linger for a while, though. We, personally, thank God that granuloma is confined almost exclusively to the Negro race.

BUDWINKLE Also it's an extremely repellent disease, with high mortality.

GLANZ Yes, sir. We sometimes shudder to think what might happen if granuloma were easily contracted by our white marines and sailor boys. God knows they are promiscuous enough as it is.

BUDWINKLE You know, Glanz, I've heard recently of a remarkable new drug, developed in England. I believe it's called penicillin. *(Puts accent on the wrong syllable)* So far it's worked miracles on all sorts of previously intractable infectious diseases. Unfortunately, I gather it won't be available to our Navy until sometime next year.

GLANZ Penicillin, sir. Yes, we've heard about the drug. Could be a godsend. But won't it offer grave problems besides, sir?

BUDWINKLE How's that, Doctor?

GLANZ Well, if it becomes the specific drug of therapy in most venereal cases, won't this open up the floodgates of vice? For if a libertine knows that he can indulge himself with impunity, he will throw all caution to the winds. What universal debauchery this might portend for our nation!

BUDWINKLE   God forbid, Dr. Glanz.

GLANZ   Meanwhile, sir, we make do, make do. Old-fashioned moral outrage simply does not seem to be sufficient. Also, we suspend the pay and allowances of these VD cases. It should be a deterrent, but it isn't. So in the end it looks as if there is absolutely nothing to prevent them from copulating like rabbits, and without even taking the precaution of using the condoms and the prophylaxis we dispense free. Free, sir! Free!

BUDWINKLE   The most powerful—I should say, the most *influential*—forces in Washington would tend to support your view, Glanz. On the other hand, there's a faction of namby-pamby and bleeding-heart liberals in the Navy department and in the government generally who'd like to try to minimize the atrocious nature of venereal disease. They'd propose to eliminate it entirely as an offense on a serviceman's record. *(Makes a mock-effeminate gesture)* Freshwater la-de-das! If you want to know my candid opinion, Glanz, and it's strictly entre nous—this faction has been heavily influenced by the thinking of Eleanor Roosevelt.

LINEWEAVER   Fall in for short-arm inspection!
(The VD patients begin to form a rank in front of their respective beds)

BUDWINKLE   We've spoken of gonorrhea. What's the situation here vis-à-vis syphilis?

GLANZ   Runs a poor second to gonorrhea, sir, but of course we get many cases. Syphilis! That bedraggled old tart still gives us lots of surprises and unless nipped in the bud is virtually incurable. For instance, only last night a lad came in—young marine of eighteen, you'll see him in a moment—with an unbelievable positive Wassermann. I'm convinced his syphilis is far advanced, but diagnosis remains doggone tough, if we might say so, sir. He disclaims having observed any of the other standard symptoms. He also refuses to admit to any promiscuity. We suspect with this particular boy it's a simple case of *lying*. His manner was very devious, we thought, and—well, frankly, he has the soft, full mouth of a voluptuary.

BUDWINKLE *(Chuckles)* It shouldn't be too hard to find the cut of *his* jib. Quite simply, it would seem to me that if you dip down into this boy's sexual history you might come up with a real bucketful of worms.

GLANZ Oh, yes, sir, the Captain is dead on target there! That's *most* essential. A detailed examination of a venereal patient's sexual profile is often the key to a successful diagnosis.

LINEWEAVER *(At the office door)* VD patients all assembled for short-arm, sir. *(Shouts to patients)* Attention on deck!

GLANZ Thank you, Lineweaver. *(They enter the ward)* Nothing has supplanted the old short-arm to determine the progress of therapy, Captain. It may seem a primitive method of examination in this advanced era, but no one has yet devised a better one.
(The patients are lined up in front of their beds. Accompanied by LINEWEAVER *and* BUDWINKLE, GLANZ *advances down the line, pausing first in front of* DADARIO*)*

LINEWEAVER *(Stares suggestively at* DADARIO*'s groin)* Well, bonjour, *big boy*. Skin it back. Squeeze it. Milk it down.

(DADARIO *goes through the motion of manipulating his penis, just as the others will*)

GLANZ   You're drying up nicely, Dadario. *(To* BUDWINKLE*)* This is a typical, run-of-the-mine, humdrum case of gonorrhea with no complications, which has responded well to sulfadiazine. Tomorrow there will likely be no urethral discharge, in which case we'll begin to take several smears and cultures for negative gonococci. Then doubtless this lucky lad will be out of here by the end of the week.

BUDWINKLE   I trust you'll walk the straight and narrow from now on out, Dadario. Try to keep that member of yours all buttoned up in your trousers where it belongs. America has a war to wage, but it sure as hell will lose the shooting match if its fighting men persist in waging that war not on the beaches but between the bedsheets. Right, Dadario?

DADARIO   Aye-aye, sir! Thank you, sir. I'll do my best, sir! *(Pauses)* Dr. Glanz, sir, I'd like to register a complaint.

GLANZ   What's that, Dadario?

DADARIO   It's Chalkley there. *(Gestures to the sick man in the next bed)* All night long he keeps hollerin', "Pearl! Pearl!" I can't sleep. It's drivin' me bats. Request permission to move to another bed somewhere else, sir.

GLANZ   *(Moving to the end of* CHALKLEY*'s bed)*   We're afraid you're just going to have to put up with that. You probably have only a few more days here. *(Glances at the stricken* CHALKLEY *and speaks in an aside to* BUDWINKLE*)* Though quite frankly, sir, we don't think anyone's going to have to put up with it for long. With this man's hypertension we'd be prepared for congestive heart failure at any moment.

LINEWEAVER *(To* STANCIK, *with a leer)* Pretty droopy today, dreamboat. Skin it back. Squeeze it. Milk it down.

GLANZ Here is a very difficult case, with continuing copious discharge and serious involvement in the vas deferens and the epididymus. Look at those flecks of blood. The sulfas just do not seem to be in any way effective, so it's hard to say how long we'll have this patient on our hands. The root cause with this man Stancik, as it is with so many others, is a rampaging libido, along with a sexual history that staggers the mind. Stancik says he first indulged in intercourse at the age of nine—

STANCIK *(Cheerfully)* Age eight, sir.

GLANZ Eight, then. And though now only twenty-four years old, he admits to carnal knowledge of nearly fifty women—

STANCIK It was sixty, sir. I told you. Remember that list I made—

GLANZ Sixty! Even more revealing! God! Sixty women, including the most depraved and debased streetwalkers in port cities from Boston to Seattle! *(His voice rises, tinged with indignation)* Is it any wonder that Nature takes ruthless revenge upon such licentiousness? Lineweaver, raise this man's dosage to a full gram of sulfathiozale every four hours.

LINEWEAVER Aye-aye, sir.
(They move on)

GLANZ *(Notices* BUDWINKLE *making a grimace of disgust as they pass by* CLARK*'s bed)* That rancid, pungent odor you smelled, sir, is characteristic of the late ulcerative stage of granuloma. Not much hope for that one, we're afraid. He was far advanced when he reported his condition. *(After* *inspecting* MC DANIEL, *he halts at* MAGRUDER*'s bed)* And here we have the syphilis we told you about. What's your name again, boy?

MAGRUDER   Magruder, sir. Private Wallace M., five-four-two-three-oh-seven, United States Marine Corps Reserve.

LINEWEAVER *(Leering)*   Not bad for a kiddie. Skin it back. Squeeze it. Milk it down.

GLANZ   No apparent discharge. This would indicate an absence of gonorrhea. So much for the lesser disease. But as for syphilis, Captain, his Wassermann is positively stratospheric. Or—ha!—should we say, stratospherically positive? Magruder, we want you to repeat in the presence of the Captain the information you gave us last night. First, you say you have never at any time noticed a chancre—a distinct ulcer or sore—on any of your private parts.

MAGRUDER   Yes, sir, that's right. Never.

GLANZ   Second, you have never been aware, in the last year or so, of a measle-like rash spreading over large parts of your body, and which might have been accompanied by a feeling of illness, or headache or sore throat or nausea?

MAGRUDER   No, never, sir.

GLANZ   So you see, Captain, he denies any acquaintance with the two symptoms which are an integral part of early syphilis. *(To* MAGRUDER*)* You told us last night that you were a college man.

MAGRUDER   I had a semester in college, sir.

GLANZ   You said you were studying English. That you wanted to be a writer, or a poet, or some kind of scribbler.

MAGRUDER   Yes, sir, I've written some short stories. And I write poetry—I try to.

GLANZ   To be a writer requires a rather highly developed capacity for observation, does it not?

MAGRUDER   I imagine so, sir.

GLANZ   *Imagine?* You know perfectly well that it does! And you—a college man with literary ambitions, a man supposed to be observant, *trained* to be observant—you still can stand there and claim that you never once observed any of these symptoms and signs?

MAGRUDER   That's right, sir.

GLANZ   *(Shakes his head)*   A very likely story. *(To* BUDWINKLE*)* Last night, sir, when we made a cursory physical examination, we noticed something which further helped ratify our conviction of the presence of syphilis. *(Elaborately dons a rubber glove and takes* MAGRUDER*'s penis between his fingers)* As you can see, the boy is circumcised, which of course is no longer a rarity at all among those of the Gentile persuasion. What *is* your faith, by the way?

MAGRUDER   I'm a Presbyterian, sir.

GLANZ   And, one might add, a *backslider*, eh, Magruder? Now notice, Captain, the small, pink, raised scar on the ventral surface right behind the corona. To our own practiced eyes—if you'll pardon the personal allusion—it looks like nothing so much as the scar left by a venereal chancre.

MAGRUDER   But I told you, sir, I've had that little scar ever since I was a kid!

GLANZ   It's the same story he told us last night. The implication being, of course, that the scar must have been the result of a somewhat less than perfect removal of the foreskin. *(Chuckles)* Another sly evasion, we're afraid.

BUDWINKLE   Well, Doctor, as everyone has come to know, it all simmers down to the age-old dilemma of a physician and his diagnosis. On the one hand: the doctor, trying only to extract the truth from the patient in order that he may most effectively employ the sacred art of healing—to treat him and make him well. On the other hand: the patient, so often guilty and devious, trying to squirm away from the truth—in this case, no doubt, because the truth would reveal a history of hanky-panky that smells like bilge water in a Shanghai junk.

MAGRUDER   But, sir! I *have* had that scar since I was a child! Ever since I began—well, *looking* at myself down there, I saw that scar! I tell you, sir, you've *got* to believe me— I've never had a *sore*—that thing you call a chancre— there *ever!*

GLANZ   Magruder, let us tell you something. Years of research by dedicated scientists have not produced our superb blood flocculation tests—the Wassermann and the Kahn—with the idea in mind that they might be discredited by some gossamer boyish fantasy. For the moment, in your case, we assume as fact the one-time presence of a chancre, just as we assume the present existence in you of syphilis.

BUDWINKLE   For heaven's sake, man, syphilis is a highly infectious disease! Belay all this guff! You can't be so indecent as to hold in callous disregard the lives of others —your fellow marines here who run the risk of being contaminated by you! In the name of God, have a little bit more simple decency!

GLANZ   Lineweaver, see that Magruder here uses the syphilitics' toilet and the syphilitics' washbasin. And also his eating utensils and tray will be specially sterilized and segregated from those of the other patients. *(To* BUDWINKLE*)* And now, sir, we want very much for you to see our laboratory. It's new and it's nifty.
(They exit stage right)

MAGRUDER   God! *(Sits on the end of his bed, head in hands, a picture of despair)* Ah, God!

LINEWEAVER   O.K., guys, you can use the head! Chow down in the mess hall in fifteen minutes!
(Except for the two gravely sick men, and also MAGRUDER *and* SCHWARTZ, *the patients grab towels and shaving gear and begin to straggle offstage, left)*

STANCIK   You lucky dog, Dadario. You'll be outa here next weekend. Tell me, what are you gonna do first? Give me three guesses.

DADARIO   No, I'll *tell* you what I'm goin' to do. I'm goin' to get a three-day pass and go to Savannah. Then I'm goin' to go to one of those seafood restaurants downtown and have a big meal of fried shrimp. Then I'm goin' to get myself started on a serious whiskey-drink all around town—

STANCIK   And then you're goin' to pick you up a broad, one of them sweet little Dixieland honeypots—

DADARIO   *No,* Stancik, for once in my life, for one single time in my life, I'm not goin' to get laid. I'm just goin' to sit there drinkin' whiskey, and I'm goin' to think of how it was back there in the clap shack, and I'll be thinkin' of you and that big, ugly, leakin' joint of yours, and for once in my life I'm goin' to be as pure as the first violet that blooms in the springtime. That's *all!*

(They exit, stage left)

MAGRUDER *(To himself)* You'd think that—something!
(Strikes his forehead in anguish) Ah, Jesus! No!

SCHWARTZ *(He is sitting nearby)* I suggest you try to stay
calm. Guys first come into this place and they panic. It's
almost like a state of shock. You should stay calm. What
you've got maybe can be cured, when they find out how
far it's gone, and so on. I know a little something about
it. I'm a hospital corpsman—O.K., a sick hospital corpsman—but I've seen plenty of guys cured for what you've
got. It depends on how far it's gone.
  (As SCHWARTZ *speaks,* LINEWEAVER *quietly takes* CHALK-
  LEY *'s blood pressure, then moves to* CLARK *'s bedside, where,
  donning a surgical mask, he pulls back the sheets to expose*
  CLARK *'s inguinal—groin—area and gives him a hypodermic injection. Pulling back the sheets releases the full
  effect of the morbid odor, and both* MAGRUDER *and*
  SCHWARTZ *react to it,* MAGRUDER *violently)*

MAGRUDER What's that stink, Schwartz?

SCHWARTZ Clark. He's a mean one, that ni—oh, I almost
said *nigger.* I never like to use that word. You know, I'm
of an oppressed minority myself. But this nigger is *evil.*
I think he's also half-crazy. He's dying. That smell. I've
almost gotten used to it.

MAGRUDER What are you in here for?

SCHWARTZ Tuberculosis of the kidney, they think I have.
A fuckin' awful disease. I've been here a long time. For
me they don't have much of a cure, if that's what's wrong
with me. At least for you they've got Dr. Ehrlich's Magic
Bullet. And that works fine a lot of times, if what you've
got hasn't progressed too far. That's why you should try
to stay calm.

MAGRUDER   What's Dr. Ehrlich's Magic Bullet?

SCHWARTZ   You mean you never saw that movie about Dr. Ehrlich's Magic Bullet? Edward G. Robinson was the star of it. A hell of a movie! I remember I saw it—

MAGRUDER   *(Impatiently)*   But the cure. What about the cure?

SCHWARTZ   The Magic Bullet? What he invented was some kind of chemical compound. Made out of arsenic or mercury, something like that. It's called 606. That's because it took Edward G. Robinson six hundred and six experiments before he found a drug that would work.

MAGRUDER   Well, how *does* it work?

SCHWARTZ   I don't know the exact way it's done. But this guy who was last here—this marine with syphilis who was here last month—they took him away to the hospital up at Bethesda. They said they were going to give him hypodermic injections for fifteen months.

MAGRUDER   God! Fifteen months. That's forever.

SCHWARTZ   Well, it beats dying. Almost anything beats dying.

MAGRUDER   *(After a long silence, rises to his feet)*   You know, it's funny, Schwartz—I don't feel sick. I feel so well! And to think *(Pauses)* to think that one reason I joined the Marine Corps was so that I'd stop worrying about my health. I mean, as a civilian I was always worried about *some* disease—like I was going to get cancer. Or T.B. Christ, T.B.! Somebody would cough in my face and all day long I'd brood about it, thinking they'd given me T.B. Or arthritis! I'd get a charley horse in swimming, and then I'd forget about it, and the next day I'd wake up in bed and feel the pain in my leg and say to myself, "Shit! I've got arthritis." Once I was sure I had an incurable growth in my neck, and I finally got up enough courage to go to the doctor, and he felt it and told me it was just one of my ligaments. But I thought I would get over that, being a marine, running around and marching and doing push-ups and so on. Only, I become a marine and what happens? I find out I've got *syphilis*. The most positive Wassermann in the history of the United States Marine Corps! Christ, I've got these millions of germs *swarming* inside me—

SCHWARTZ   Spirochetes.

MAGRUDER   What did you say?

SCHWARTZ   Not *germs* inside you. Fuckin' *spirochetes*. That's what they're called. I've seen them in a microscope.

MAGRUDER   What's the difference?

SCHWARTZ   Germs look like—well, *germs*. Little rods and balls and globs and such. Syphilis spirochetes look like tiny little fuckin' corkscrews.

MAGRUDER   *(With a small shudder)*   Jesus! Corkscrews! Billions of them!

SCHWARTZ   That's right. Billions of them. That's what makes syphilis different.

MAGRUDER   But Schwartz, listen, I *couldn't* have gotten syphilis! Because I—it's impossible! *(Pauses)* Well, I'm not really a virgin. I have had women—*two* of them. But they —no! I mean, I must have picked it up from a toilet seat or something.

LINEWEAVER   *(Approaches, holding a white robe, and sarcastically picks up on* MAGRUDER*'s last line)*   Ho! Ho! Ho! A toilet seat! That's the oldest joke in the book, dopey. You couldn't get what you've got from a toilet seat if you slept with one every night for a year.

MAGRUDER   Then I must have gotten it in some mess hall or someplace, where the dishes and silver and things weren't washed properly—

LINEWEAVER   Wally, let me give you some good advice. Stop blaming inanimate objects for your problems. Syphilis is contracted in one way—through sex-u-al in-tercourse. Accept the fact that you're a very fancy fornicator —there's hardly any shame in that, after all—and that what happened to you could have happened to any dedicated whoremonger.

MAGRUDER   But that's just the point, don't you see? If I were some—what you call fancy fornicator, I'd understand! But I—

LINEWEAVER   *(Ignoring his words)*   You'll be using this robe instead of the one you're wearing. As you can see, it has a yellow "S" stitched to the breast, to identify your disease.

MAGRUDER   I can't wear that! Jesus, it's like—it's like *The Scarlet Letter!*

LINEWEAVER   *(Insistently)*   Yes, I think you *will* wear it, Wally. Dr. Glanz's rules.

MAGRUDER   When do I have to wear it?

LINEWEAVER   All the time on the ward, and whenever you go anywhere else in the hospital—to the mess hall, say, or to the movies, or the library.

MAGRUDER   *(Indignantly)*   Maybe you should give me a bell to ring, too! Like some—like some *leper!*

LINEWEAVER   Another thing. When you go to the head, you
must use the toilet on the extreme right. It's plainly
marked with a yellow "S," just like the washbasin you
have to use.

MAGRUDER   If you say you can't pick it up from a toilet seat,
why all the fuss about giving me a special one?

LINEWEAVER   It's simply a matter of *order*—so you'll get
used to your new status.

MAGRUDER   I'll never get used to my new status. Never!

LINEWEAVER   Don't look so *glum*, Wally! After all, the clap
patients have *their* separate facilities. We just don't want
to mix up the gonococci with the spirochetes. A matter
of order, that's all.

MAGRUDER   *(Looking at the letter on the robe)*   "S." It's yellow.
A particularly repulsive shade of yellow. *(Turns to*
SCHWARTZ*)* Why yellow? It makes me feel like—
        (He halts)

SCHWARTZ   Yes, Wally?
        (He exchanges a significant look with MAGRUDER*)*

MAGRUDER   *(Puts on the robe)*   Yes! Exactly! *(Strikes his forehead)* God almighty!

LINEWEAVER   *(As* DR. GLANZ *and* CAPTAIN BUDWINKLE *return
from stage right)*   Attention on deck!
        *(*MAGRUDER *and* SCHWARTZ *stand at attention as the two
        officers pass through the ward)*

BUDWINKLE   A splendid lab, Dr. Glanz, perfectly splendid.
Great little gadgets! I especially am taken by those Kraft-
Stekel monoprecipitators. *(Chuckles)* I'll bet they set the
Navy back a pretty penny.

GLANZ *(Also chuckles appreciatively)*   In the neighborhood of six of the "big bills," we should say, sir.

> *(As they talk, the other patients—who have been at their morning ablutions—straggle back onstage. At this moment* CHALKLEY *gives a loud, agonized moan from his bed.* LINE-WEAVER *rushes to his side, scrutinizes his face closely as he feels the man's pulse. He then hurries to the door at stage right)*

LINEWEAVER *(Shouts)*   Anderson! Smith! On the double here! Oxygen! *Adrenalin!* Hurry, I say! Chop-chop!

BUDWINKLE *(Oblivious of the pandemonium)*   It is too bad, however, Doctor, that you don't have a Banghart twin-speed pressure pump for reverse catheterizations. They're damned useful in a pinch.

GLANZ   Well, such a lack, sir, does indeed sorely trouble the heart of a deeply involved urologist like ourself. We hope and pray the Captain will put one on order.

> *(While they have been talking, center stage,* LINEWEAVER *has run back to* CHALKLEY*'s side, closely followed now by two hospital corpsmen,* ANDERSON *and* SMITH, *who are bearing with them the lifesaving paraphernalia that* LINE-WEAVER *has called for. As the three corpsmen huddle around the stricken man and apply their various instruments, the two officers continue to talk)*

BUDWINKLE   I'll try, I'll try. Well, it was an illuminating tour, Doctor. Your ward is about as shipshape as such a pesthole can get, and I congratulate you.

GLANZ   Thank you, sir. We always try to do our best.

BUDWINKLE   Keep me closely posted on your two terminal cases. Also that boy with syphilis. I'd especially like to know what you'll dredge up out of *that* rat's nest.

(While BUDWINKLE *speaks,* SCHWARTZ *has drawn close to* CLARK*'s bed, and he and the recumbent Negro are gazing intently at the frenzied, quiet activity of the three men at* CHALKLEY*'s bedside)*

MAGRUDER *(In a panicky voice)* What's he dying of, Schwartz?

SCHWARTZ It's some kind of nephritis, a kidney disease.

GLANZ Aye-aye, sir. It shouldn't be too long before we've developed a most revealing sexual profile.

MAGRUDER Nephritis! *(Gives a shudder)* Jesus, you don't suppose it's contagious, do you? *(Backs away)* This place is a *charnel house!*

BUDWINKLE Thank you, Doctor! Smooth cruising! And keep up the good work!
(He exits stage right, while GLANZ, *basking in the praise, stands with his back to the tense episode on stage. The lights fade)*

Around noontime of the same day. The routine now is similar to that of the early morning. Except for the two bedridden patients, the occupants of the ward are clad in robes. A couple loll about on their beds. Others sit on chairs reading, for the most part comic books. A portable radio plays "Frenesi" and other tunes of the swing music era. One or two of the patients—including MA-GRUDER, *whose bed is next to* CLARK*'s—are reading or writing letters.* ANDERSON, *a hospital corpsman, sits attentively next to* CHALKLEY*'s bed, occasionally administering oxygen and monitoring the condition of the critically ill patient. As they attend to their various activities, a personage in the vestments of a* CATHOLIC CHAPLAIN *enters stage left and approaches* LINEWEAVER, *who has entered from stage right and who at this moment is hovering over* CHALKLEY*'s bed. The* CHAPLAIN *is accompanied by a young assistant bearing the equipment used in the last rites of the Church.*

CHAPLAIN (*To* LINEWEAVER) I was told that there was a man here who required the last rites.

LINEWEAVER I don't think so, sir.

CHAPLAIN (*Looking somberly at* CHALKLEY) Why? This man is clearly gravely ill.

LINEWEAVER Well, *that's* for sure, sir. He's in a coma. He couldn't be any sicker.

CHAPLAIN *(Moving forward)* Then I shall certainly administer extreme unction.

LINEWEAVER But, sir, the man's a Baptist.

CHAPLAIN He couldn't be a Baptist.

LINEWEAVER Pardon me, sir, but he is. He told me. Besides, it's on his dog tags. "P" for Protestant.

CHAPLAIN Listen, this is impossible. I received a message from regimental headquarters saying that a Catholic will be dying on B Ward.

LINEWEAVER But, sir, this is D Ward.

CHAPLAIN You mean, this is not B for Baker Ward?

LINEWEAVER No, sir. D for Dog Ward.

CHAPLAIN D for Dog?

LINEWEAVER Yessir. B Ward's orthopedic.

CHAPLAIN Then what's this?

LINEWEAVER Urological and venereal.

CHAPLAIN Urological and venereal? *(Shudders)* Heavens! *(To the* ASSISTANT, *briskly)* Come along, Wilkins! Quickly! Quickly!
> *(He hurries offstage left and exits, trailed by the* ASSISTANT *with his equipment. At extreme stage left is the bed of a young marine named* McDANIEL, *who has been avidly re-reading the letter he has just received. He rises suddenly from his chair, and his voice arrests the attention of the other patients)*

McDANIEL I don't believe it! I just don't believe it!

DADARIO   What happened, McDaniel? You gettin' surveyed out of the service?

McDANIEL   It's a letter—I mean a personal letter—from Rhonda Fleming's personal secretary!

STANCIK   What did Rhonda say, McDaniel? Does she want to blow you?

McDANIEL *(With real reproof)*   Cut it out, you creep! You're not fit to utter her name! *(Returns to the letter)* Listen to this. "Dear Davy: Like all screen stars, Miss Fleming receives hundreds of fan letters every day, and she could not possibly answer them herself. But you write her so often that she's terribly impressed, and she wanted me to send you this personal message. She thinks marines like you are the finest, cleanest, bravest boys in America, and she hopes you'll be thinking of her when you go overseas and slap that Jap. Sincerely yours . . ."
   (His voice trails off in awe)

STANCIK   I'll bet she'd shit if she knew you had the clap.

McDANIEL *(Advances angrily on* STANCIK*)*   Listen, you jerk, I've had just about enough out of you—

LINEWEAVER *(Moves between them)*   Come, come, no rough-house, boys! It's twelve o'clock. Time for chow! *(To all)* Chow down, you guys! All except you, Schwartz. You've got a stomach exam this afternoon.
   (The patients exit stage left, leaving MAGRUDER *sitting on the chair by his bed,* SCHWARTZ *near him. The* HOSPITAL CORPSMEN *leave the bedside of* CHALKLEY, *who lies breathing under oxygen.* LINEWEAVER *looks back from extreme stage left)*

LINEWEAVER   No chow for you, sonny boy?

MAGRUDER   No, I'm—I just don't seem to have any appetite. I'll just stay here, if it's O.K.

LINEWEAVER *(Rather sympathetically):*   Sure, Wally. I understand. Lots of guys lose their appetite when they first come in here. You'll get it back.
>   (LINEWEAVER *exits.* MAGRUDER *sits reading one of the letters for a moment.* CLARK, *silent and propped against the pillows, gazes with the listlessness of one who is very sick at* MAGRUDER and SCHWARTZ)

SCHWARTZ *(His voice touched with envy and admiration)*   You got a lot of letters.

MAGRUDER *(Self-deprecatingly)*   Oh—well, yes, I guess I did. Five. I guess that's a lot for one day.

SCHWARTZ   I only got one, but at least I get one almost every day. From my wife. That's something. It makes you feel less lonesome. Who'd you get your letters from?

MAGRUDER   My girl, she's in my home town in Virginia. Sometimes she writes me a couple times—more!—maybe three times a day. Mainly she writes me about the books she's been reading. She's very big on poetry, like I am.

SCHWARTZ   She a blonde or brunette?

MAGRUDER   Sort of in between, I guess you'd say. Chestnut brown, would that be the right description? Yeah, chestnut brown.

SCHWARTZ   Has she got a nice build?

MAGRUDER *(With feeling)*   She's got *everything.*

SCHWARTZ   I wish my wife had everything. Her face, it's nice. It looks a little like—well, she looks a little bit like Ava Gardner. But the rest of her—the build—it's gone to fat. It's a shame. *(Pauses)* Chestnut brown. I like that color. I like poetry, too.

MAGRUDER *(With spirit)*   You do? What poets have you read?

SCHWARTZ   Oh, I don't read much poetry. I read books though. Constructive books. *(Gestures at two books nearby)* Things that are valuable and you can really get your teeth into.

MAGRUDER   What books are they?

SCHWARTZ   Well, this one is called *How To Manage a Pet Shop*. After the war I'm going to buy a pet shop. I like animals—dogs, cats, birds, turtles, snakes even. I'd love to have a pet shop. Then this other book is called *(Reading title) Tolerance for Others, or How to Develop Human Compassion*, by Rabbi Max Weinberg of Temple Rodef Sholem, Cincinnati, Ohio. What a book! What a fuckin' marvelous book!

MAGRUDER   It sounds interesting. Impressive. What's it all about?

SCHWARTZ   Well, mainly it's about suffering.

MAGRUDER   How do you mean?

SCHWARTZ   Well, he tells about how in my *(Hesitates)*—in my *ethnic*, our people have borne unspeakable oppression for many thousands of years. Listen—*(Begins to read)* "Persecuted, enslaved, the *poor* victims of—"

CLARK *(Interrupting)*   Poor! Hee-hee! Poor! Dat do grab my black ass! *Rich*, you means! De Jew ain't poor, de Jew is *rich!* De Jew is rich like de First National Bank of Memphis. De Jew is *poor?* Hee-hee! Dat is plain, ordinary *mu-ule* shit! Ole Man Klein in my hometown of Bolivar, Tennessee, dat Jew so rich he pee into a solid gold pisspot. Dat "poor" jive! Dat *do* grab my ass!

(Falls back with a sigh)

SCHWARTZ *(With great patience)* Just ignore that nigger. He's evil, that one. Anyway, to answer your question further, what he says in this book, *Tolerance for Others*, is that since the Jewish people have endured so much suffering, they must comprehend the suffering of others and be what he calls the standard bearers in the march for human compassion. *(Pauses, reads)* "There is one lesson for humanity: people must love one another."

CLARK Hee-hee! Dat is *mule shit!*

MAGRUDER *(After a pause)* Well, what do you mean about liking poetry, Schwartz?

SCHWARTZ What I mean by liking it is, I like the idea of poetry *being* there—for people who like it.

MAGRUDER Then didn't you ever read any poetry?

SCHWARTZ Sure. I recited a poem out loud when I graduated from high school. I won a prize for it, too! *(Glumly, after a pause)* A framed picture of the superintendent of the Board of Education.

MAGRUDER What was the poem?

SCHWARTZ "Crossing the Bar," by Tennyson. I still know it by heart. *(Pauses)* "Sunset and evening star, and one clear call for me. And may there be no moaning at the bar, when I put out to sea . . ." *(Pauses, reflects)* That's beautiful poetry, isn't it? And sad. It's about dying.

MAGRUDER Well, yes. *(Hesitantly)* It *is* beautiful, but—but there's other poetry that does so much more to me. I mean, have you ever read T.S. Eliot?

CLARK T.S. Eliot. Eliot, *T.S.* Dat means *tough shit* for Eliot. Tee-hee!

SCHWARTZ   Shut up! Go on, Wally. Who is this poet?

MAGRUDER   T.S. Eliot. He's a great poet. He's fantastic! And then there's Emily Dickinson, and Hart Crane, and Wallace Stevens. Stevens! He writes pure music! There's this passage of his—it's about dying, too—that goes like this: "The body dies; the body's beauty lives . . . So evenings die . . . in their green going, a wave . . . interminably flowing." *(Pauses)* And you want to know something, Schwartz? This guy Stevens is the vice-president of an insurance company up in Hartford, Connecticut!

SCHWARTZ   *(Ruminatively)* "The body dies; the body's beauty lives." That's *good*. He writes good poetry. And you say he's in insurance? What did you say his name is —Eliot?

MAGRUDER   Stevens. Wallace Stevens. I'd give anything to be able to write lines of poetry like that.

SCHWARTZ   "The body dies; the body's beauty lives." *(Long pause)* They're running a stomach test on me this afternoon. On top of my kidney thing, Dr. Glanz thinks I might have developed some kind of an ulcer.

MAGRUDER   God, I'm sorry about that.

SCHWARTZ   You can't win! You have T.B. of the kidney and you worry about that until you get an ulcer. Now I'm worried about my ulcer.

CLARK   *(He has been gazing at* MAGRUDER *and* SCHWARTZ, *and now his sudden giggle startles them again)*   Hee-hee! *(There is a sick lassitude in his laugh, and his voice is spiritless, enervated)* Hee-hee! Dat poetry jive! Dat is some kind of funny! You white boys so full of shit hit runnin' clean out yo' ears.

MAGRUDER What's *wrong* with him?

SCHWARTZ He's a mean one, that *schwarze.* I think he's half
out of his mind. It's that sickness of his.

CLARK Ain't never listened to such dumb, low-down white
boys' *mule shit* in all my life. Hee-hee! Dat is sho some
kind of funny. *(Rises slowly on his elbow)* Po-etry! Dat do
grab my black ass!

MAGRUDER *(Placatingly)* Gee, I didn't mean—

SCHWARTZ Don't pay any attention to him. He's a menace.
Shut your face, Lorenzo! *(In an aside)* I've gotta have
tolerance! *(In an unctuous tone)* Just try to sleep.

CLARK Ain't studyin' about no sleep, Jew-boy.

SCHWARTZ He's *filled* with hate. Once—before you came
here—I had a visit from my wife. Only when she arrived
I wasn't on the ward at the moment. Then when Clark
saw her, he told her that I had died.

MAGRUDER That's awful!

CLARK De Man *(Gestures weakly to heaven)* de *Man* gwine
shut *my* face soon enough. And I'll get sleep. And you too,
Jew-boy. Because you and me—us gwine *die!*

SCHWARTZ *(Shudders)* I can't stand it!

MAGRUDER What's *wrong* with him?

CLARK *(To MAGRUDER)* Likewise you dere too, white boy,
you wid dat sy-philis. Hee! hee! Dey gwine carry you outa
here in a wooden kee-mo-no.

SCHWARTZ I'm goin' to get Lineweaver to shut him up. *(In
a sudden rage)* You stink to heaven, Lorenzo! Fuck tolerance! Fuck you too, Lorenzo!

CLARK   I *do* stink and I *is* black, and I is po' as Job's turkey,
and I isn't got any kinfolk to mou'n me to my grave. But
one thing I does know is dat dere ain't no difference
between a dead nigger and a dead Jew-boy when dey is
both food for de worms. *Equal!*
   (Sinks back, depleted, breathing heavily)

SCHWARTZ   Why do you hate so? *(CLARK does not reply)* I've
never done a fuckin' thing to you! *(To MAGRUDER)* I've
only tried to be friendly to him.

MAGRUDER   Maybe you're right. Maybe that sickness has
gotten to his brain.

SCHWARTZ   I can't think of anything else. *(Suddenly MA-
GRUDER leaps to his feet, standing rigidly erect at the end of his
bed)* What's wrong?

MAGRUDER *(In great agitation)*   Jesus Christ, I feel like I've
died and waked up in hell! This place is driving me ape-
shit!

SCHWARTZ   Take it easy, Wally!
   *(As SCHWARTZ attempts to calm him, a light goes up in
   GLANZ's office, and GLANZ appears—this time garbed in a
   doctor's white jacket. Simultaneously, LINEWEAVER appears at extreme stage left)*

LINEWEAVER   Magruder! Dr. Glanz wants you for an examination.

SCHWARTZ *(To MAGRUDER, as he crosses the stage)*   Good luck,
Wally.
   (MAGRUDER enters GLANZ's office and stands at attention)

MAGRUDER   Private Magruder, Wallace M., five-four-two-
three-oh-seven, reporting as ordered, sir.

GLANZ *(Fiddles with papers, without looking up from the desk
where he is seated)*   At ease, Magruder. Sit down. *(MA-*

GRUDER *takes a chair opposite the doctor, who continues to shuffle ostentatiously through his papers, then finally looks up)* We'll come directly to the point, Magruder. Despite the famous toilet-seat myth, syphilis is *always* contracted through sexual intercourse. Consequently, following a clinical examination such as you have already received, a thorough and meticulous history must be made of a patient's sexual activities. You understand the logic of this, do you not?

MAGRUDER   Yes, sir.

GLANZ   Very well. It is not our intention, today, to obtain from you this sexual profile in detail. That will come in due course. However, we do want to take the first preliminary steps. Let us then ask you this. With how many women have you had sexual congress?
(Begins to make notes)

MAGRUDER   In my entire life, sir?

GLANZ   In your entire life.

MAGRUDER   Two women, sir.

GLANZ   *(After a long pause and a penetrating gaze)*   Magruder, look at us. Look at us carefully. Can you do that?

MAGRUDER   I am looking at you—at you all—carefully, sir.

GLANZ   You see that we are a grown man of middle age, father of four children, medical training in Budapest, Guy's Hospital, London, University of Arkansas, member of the American Medical Association, fellow of the American College of Urological Surgeons, listed in *Who's Who in America*, a practitioner of the art of medicine for twenty-five years. You see before you a man of large experience, and we hope, at this late date, of some wisdom. No less and no more than any of our patients, we suffer. If you prick us, we too will say "Ouch." In short,

3 5

you see a very deeply human human being. *(Pauses)* All the more reason, then, that we feel that we are endowed with insight. Therefore what you do *not* see, on the other hand, is an innocent. What you do *not* see, Magruder, is a sucker. You do not see a callow, gullible young intern eager to swallow any harebrained invention that might pass a patient's lips. Do you expect us then to believe that you have had intercourse with *only two* women?

MAGRUDER *(Emphatically)* Yes, sir, because it's a fact.

GLANZ Preposterous.

MAGRUDER Well, sir, can't you see? There hasn't been enough time. I'm sorry! I'm just eighteen!

GLANZ You're young, it's true, but most of those fellow marines of yours—no older than you and in your same fix —have confessed to relations with women by the *score*. Regrettably, there is no truth serum available to elicit the real facts from you. *(Sighs)* Though we are convinced that you lie, we have no alternative but to take you at your word. *(Pauses, gazes intently into* MAGRUDER*'s eyes)* Only two, you say. Just who were these—these females?

MAGRUDER One of them was—*(He falters, embarrassed)* She was—

GLANZ Come, come, Magruder. You must have no hesitancy about these matters. Can't you understand? We are recording these details so that we can try to *save your life!*

MAGRUDER She was an older woman, sir.

GLANZ An older woman. Would you mind telling us how many times you had physical contact with this older woman?

MAGRUDER Once, sir. Only once.

GLANZ   All it *takes* is once. And the other—female. Who was she?

MAGRUDER   She's my—well, she's my *girl*, sir.

GLANZ   You speak of her in the present tense. We assume this means that you have recently had relations with this girl of yours, and/or continue to have such relations.

MAGRUDER   That's right, sir.

GLANZ   She's how old?

MAGRUDER   She's just my age, sir. Eighteen. Well, a bit younger. Seventeen-and-a-half.

GLANZ   May we ask how many times you have had sexual contact with this girl?

MAGRUDER   *(A long pause)*   Oh, gee, sir, I wouldn't know. I would have lost count. Many, many times. Maybe hundreds. I've been in love with her for two years or more.

GLANZ   *(Arises and goes to one wall of the office, where he pulls down a huge chart or diagram, a grotesque cartoon which is clearly that of the human brain)*   Hundreds, eh, Magruder? We'd say you've got a pretty athletic little romance going there. *(Gestures toward chart)* Do you know what this is?

MAGRUDER   Well, sir, it looks like a kind of map, or medical chart or something, of the brain.

GLANZ   Precisely. A diagram of that grandest and most complex of organs, the human brain.

MAGRUDER   It certainly *looks* complex, sir.

GLANZ   *The brain.* It may be the most majestic creation of the deity. It is here that it originates, Magruder, the ineffable mystery of *thought*—that miraculous process which has allowed mankind to produce its real standouts: a

Henry Ford, say, or a musical prodigy like John Philip Sousa, or professional heroes in our own pantheon, like Rudolf Wachter, the father of bladder surgery. A noble machine, would you not agree?

MAGRUDER Yes, sir.

GLANZ Yet a machine subject to malfunction, to bugs, gremlins, to breakdown—like all machines. In short, a mechanism subject to *disease*. *(Pauses)* Magruder, did you ever hear of the word paresis?

MAGRUDER No, sir.

GLANZ You have no idea, then, what paresis means, or what the definition of paretic is?

MAGRUDER No, I'm afraid I don't, sir.

GLANZ To be paretic is to have paresis. Paresis in turn is a neurological form of syphilis which affects the brain.

MAGRUDER *(Anxiety in his voice now)* How does it affect the brain, sir?

GLANZ *(Takes a pointer in hand)* It creates an inflammatory process, known as meningoencephalitis. This inflammation may appear on any brain area but tends to localize *(Indicates with pointer)* here at the basal aspect. Or here at the frontal aspect.

MAGRUDER Well, sir, what happens to someone when this takes place?

GLANZ The patient becomes insane. *(Pauses)* Stark, raving mad. *(Long pause)* Loony as a dingbat.

MAGRUDER *(Gasps)* Jesus! Sir.

GLANZ Let us ask you something else, Magruder. Have you ever heard of locomotor ataxia?

MAGRUDER No, sir. What's that?

GLANZ Locomotor ataxia is another form of neurosyphilis. It affects the posterior columns of the spinal cord *(Uses pointer)* here, and certain cranial nerves, here and here, including the optic nerve, here.

MAGRUDER And what happens with this, sir?

GLANZ The patient becomes unable to walk properly. Then he goes blind. He also finally becomes hopelessly paralyzed.

MAGRUDER My God!
　(Begins, almost unconsciously, to feel himself, arms and legs)

GLANZ It's a bitch of a disease, Magruder, we'll tell you. *(Pauses, rolls the chart back up so that it snaps like a window shade, sits down once again)* You may think that we have shown you all this in order to alarm you, but we can assure you that this has not been our intention.

MAGRUDER I hope you'll pardon me for saying so, sir, but it sure *does* alarm me. God—I'm alarmed!

GLANZ We've done this not to alarm you but to shock you into an awareness of the seriousness of your condition. Also to impress upon you the necessity for perfect honesty and candor on your part in any discussion the two of us will have in regard to your sexual history. The evidence now speaks for itself. You must have chosen to ignore the early symptoms—the chancre and the rash. Therefore we are forced inescapably to believe that you have passed out of the primary and secondary stages of syphilis and are now passing into the last—the tertiary stage. While ordinarily the grave conditions I've described to you take a number of years to develop, there is a form of the disease which is not uncommon called "galloping syphilis," in which the patient is quickly over-whelmed by paresis or locomotor ataxia, or both. It is *this* that we are concerned about in your case. *(Pauses)* Alas, also the possibility of—*(He shrugs)*

MAGRUDER *(In a real panic)* Then doesn't this mean I'm going to *die?* Isn't that what you're saying, sir? That I'm going to get all these things you've been describing? Jesus, sir, isn't there any hope for me? Any at all!

GLANZ *(Disarmed for the first time, he softens a little bit and his voice loses some of its harshness)* No, no, Magruder! Calm yourself, boy! There's no *certainty* in any of this!

MAGRUDER *(Almost in tears)* But you make it sound so cer-tain, sir! God, I don't want to go crazy! Get paralyzed, go blind! I'd rather *die!*

GLANZ We insist that you calm yourself! We can under-stand this self-concern in you. It is normal of you to have this fear. But you must remember that we have drugs which are sometimes effective in arresting this disease. *(Smiles thinly)* Unless, of course, it has progressed *too far.*

MAGRUDER Six-o-six? The Magic Bullet? Fifteen months of injections?

GLANZ For a layman, you have a rare expertise, Magruder. Yes, that drug has been used with some success. Keep that in mind. We want you to leave this office in an optimistic mood. And now you're dismissed.

> (MAGRUDER, *weak and shaken, rises, does an about-face and walks toward the office door*)

GLANZ Oh, Magruder.

MAGRUDER *(Abruptly turning)* Sir?

GLANZ *(Raises the thumb of his right hand in a gesture of bonhomie and palship)* Chin up, there!

(MAGRUDER *walks, shaken, dejectedly across the ward to the place by his bed.* SCHWARTZ *looks up from his book*)

SCHWARTZ   How did it go, Wally?

MAGRUDER   Terrible, Schwartz. Terrible! It couldn't have gone worse. *(Pauses, wondering)* I mean, that *Glanz!* He's, he's a—
      (He halts)

SCHWARTZ   Don't let Dr. Glanz get *to* you like that, Wally. He's well-known for always wanting people to be sick. It's what's known as a personality quirk, I think.

MAGRUDER *(Taking out of his footlocker a piece of writing paper and a fountain pen)*   Well, Schwartz, he *did* get to me. He did get to me, that son of a bitch!
      (He begins to write, and as he writes, for a minute or so a portable radio is heard, playing a strange mélange of hillbilly music, scraps of hit songs of the period, a brief insane passage from Bach's St. Matthew Passion, *war reports from the Pacific, announcing huge marine casualties at Tarawa. Finally he breaks off writing, places pen and paper down and slowly rises to his feet. He is greatly agitated)*

SCHWARTZ   Writing to the little sweetheart, I'll bet. You hurt my conscience, Wally. I owe my wife a letter for over a week. *(With a look of revulsion,* MAGRUDER *tears the letter to pieces. At this,* SCHWARTZ *rises too)* What's wrong? Take it easy! Listen, don't panic!

MAGRUDER *(Cries out in the direction of* GLANZ'*s office)*   You're not going to get *me,* Dr. Glanz! I'm not going to *die* in this stinking, misbegotten, low-down *kennel* of yours. You hear me, Dr. Glanz?

SCHWARTZ   Quiet, Wally! *Quiet!* You can't *do* that! If he ever heard you, he'd punish the whole ward! Quiet!

MAGRUDER *(Calmer now)* But I can't *stand* this place! It's going to drive me absolutely crackers!

SCHWARTZ You just have to have courage, Wally. Courage! Like Rabbi Weinberg says, the handmaiden of tolerance is *courage.*

CLARK *(Rising up on his elbow)* Courage! Tee-hee! Dat is some kind of mule shit!

SCHWARTZ *(Turning in a rage)* Shut up! God, you stink to-day! I can't stand the way you smell, it's worse than ever! Why don't you die? *(Wrings his hands, averting his eyes)* Forgive me. Tolerance!

CLARK *(Weakly)* It ain't *me* dat stink so bad. *(Gestures in the direction of* CHALKLEY*'s bed)* Why don't you take you a whiff of *him?* He *stone dead,* smellin' like a ole catfish all mornin'. *(Pauses)* Food for de worms. *Equal!*

> *(His laughter dominates the scene.* MAGRUDER, SCHWARTZ *and, more slowly, the other patients on the ward turn and gaze silently at* CHALKLEY*'s inert form as the lights go down on the stage)*

ACT TWO

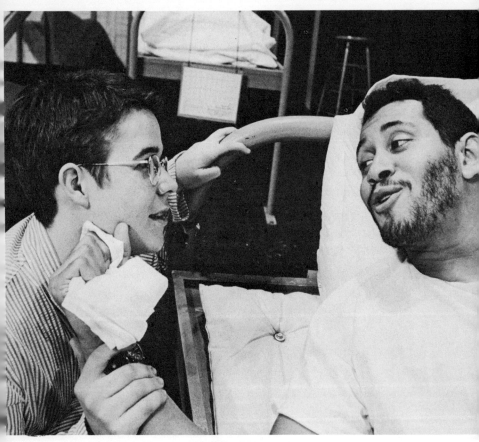

Miles Chapin as MAGRUDER and Hannibal
Penney, Jr., as LORENZO CLARK.

It is a week later, in the hour of the morning before reveille.
LINEWEAVER *is absent from his desk and most of the patients are*
asleep. MAGRUDER, *however, stirs slowly awake and sits on the edge*
of his bed. Soon SCHWARTZ *awakens too, and sits up erect in bed,*
yawning and stretching.

MAGRUDER   What time is it?

SCHWARTZ   It's a little after six. Reveille's in half an hour.
(Yawns) I'm so tired! For some reason I couldn't sleep.

MAGRUDER *(Yawns too)*   Where's Lineweaver?

SCHWARTZ   I can't say for sure, but I suspect he's doping
off. Asleep. He comes in from an all-night liberty and
goes to sleep in the laboratory. Once one morning I
peeked in there, and there he was—snoozing like a baby
among the urine specimens and the Bunsen burners. Boy,
if Dr. Glanz ever caught him at that!

MAGRUDER *(Yawns again, almost painfully)*   I couldn't really
sleep either. Tossed and turned all night long, filled with
these strange dreams.

SCHWARTZ   They must have been bad, Wally. You kept
groaning and talking in your sleep. I couldn't understand
anything you said—except one word. Ha! That was
funny!

MAGRUDER What word did I say?

SCHWARTZ You know what you said? You said, "Vladivostok."

MAGRUDER "Vladivostok!" Why would I say a thing like that?

SCHWARTZ I don't know, Wally. Maybe it's because you were dreaming about it. Vladivostok, that's in Russia, isn't it? I mean it's so *far away* from *here!* It's probably what Rabbi Weinberg calls a wish-fulfillment dream. *(Reaches for the book)* You know, the Rabbi has an answer for almost any problem. Here, let me read you—

MAGRUDER No Rabbi this morning, Schwartz! No more Weinberg! Please! Jesus, I've got to get out of this place!

SCHWARTZ Take it easy, Wally. Take it easy. You're not the only one stuck in this fuckin' place!
    (Approaches MAGRUDER *as if to calm him, and then coughs)*

MAGRUDER Don't get too close, Schwartz. Get away!

SCHWARTZ *(Soothingly)* Wally, Wally, you can't catch my T.B. when I cough! It's in my *kidney!* Calm down now. Take it easy! Just get hold of yourself, Wally!

MAGRUDER *(In sudden, intense embarrassment)* I'm sorry, Schwartz. I really am. I'm ashamed of myself. Jesus, if I don't die of locomotor ataxia I'll die of hypochondria. *(Pauses)* But that's just it! You know, Schwartz, if I just had some *knowledge* I might be able to make it. *Knowledge* might make me able to get through this. I mean, for instance, I had another blood test yesterday. The idea scares me. I mean, I don't know anything about blood tests. I'm a medical idiot.

SCHWARTZ You mean you really want to know *more* about what you've got? If you'll forgive me, Wally, I'd say that when it comes to syphilis, ignorance is bliss.

MAGRUDER No, I want some information about this disease I've got. Something that might show me what to look for —what symptoms, what signs! Some information that could even give me a little hope—like knowing that the disease might have, well, *stabilized* itself and maybe wasn't going to get any worse. I try to worm a little knowledge out of Dr. Glanz, but I can't even get a word of consolation from him, much less any facts. All he seems to care about is taking my what he calls sexual profile. Jesus, I forgot! I've got another one of those sexual profile sessions with him today. What a *jerk!*

SCHWARTZ Yes, sir, I'll have to agree to one thing. That Dr. Glanz is a tough cookie.

MAGRUDER *(In a sudden fury)* That's an understatement if I ever heard one, Schwartz! Tough cookie! Why, sometimes I think he's hardly made of flesh! I thought doctors were supposed to make you feel *better,* not make you feel like some worm, some worthless piece of *slime!* He's incredible! He's a *troglodyte!*

SCHWARTZ But, you know, I get to thinking: sometimes doctors have to *act* hard, tough. To protect themselves. They see so much pain, so much suffering. Actually, I'll bet Dr. Glanz is—well, very tolerant and also deeply human.

MAGRUDER Deeply human! For God's sake, that's what *he* said! Don't make me puke, Schwartz! Tolerant? Stop it! Your Jewish compassion is showing! He's a pluperfect prick! I'd like to kick him in the teeth! *(Pauses)* Yet he scares me. That I must admit.

SCHWARTZ *(Suddenly inspired)* Hey, I got an idea!

MAGRUDER An idea about what?

SCHWARTZ About that knowledge—that information you were talking about.

MAGRUDER What do you mean?

SCHWARTZ Books! In Dr. Glanz's office. There are all sorts of textbooks on your disease that could tell you everything you want to know.

MAGRUDER Yeah, but, Schwartz, since when did doctors start distributing medical textbooks to sick people?

SCHWARTZ *(His voice conspiratorial now)* No, I don't mean that. I mean we just *borrow* a book for a little while. *(Gets out of bed)* Look, the office is open. Lineweaver's asleep. It'll be easy as pie, Wally!
(Begins to move toward the office)

MAGRUDER Wait, Schwartz, you'd better not! You'll get ten years in the Portsmouth brig if Lineweaver or someone catches you stealing one of those books!

SCHWARTZ *(Insistently)* He'll never miss it if I take it just for a little while. I'll put it back right away, sometime when he's not there. *(Heads toward the office in a hurried tiptoe past the sleeping patients)* Don't worry, Wally!
(While SCHWARTZ exits, CLARK stirs in his bed. As on the earlier morning, we are made aware that the black man has been closely attending the previous conversation, silently listening to every word)

CLARK *(His voice weak and strained as usual)* How is de syphilis dis mawnin'?

MAGRUDER *(Truly startled)* WHAT!

CLARK Hush, man! You gwine rouse up de whole hospital. How come you jump like dat?
(At stage left, in GLANZ*'s office,* SCHWARTZ *takes a book from a shelf and begins to read, underlining certain passages with a pencil)*

MAGRUDER *(Recovering himself)* You startled me! I mean— well, it's the first thing you've said to me since the day I came into this place. I didn't expect it, that's all. I was startled.

CLARK *(Makes his cracked little laugh)* You looks better, white boy. Not so peak-ed roun' de jowls. I 'spect you might even live fo' a while—befo' you gits et up by dem *spiral- keets.*

MAGRUDER Don't make jokes like that. Jokes about *that*— in this place—they're not funny. *(Turns away)* You might as well get this straight: I'm not going to take any shit off you, Lorenzo. I'm not going to be another Schwartz. I'm not going to be another scapegoat for your misery.

CLARK No, listen, white boy, I wants to tell you somethin'. *(Halts, then continues to speak laboriously)* I *likes* you, I truly likes you—

MAGRUDER I don't want you to like me! *(Resentfully)* Stay off my back, Lorenzo! Leave me the fuck alone!

CLARK But I *does* like you! Likewise, I does *not* like de Jew-boy. I likes you all right. You wants to know why?

MAGRUDER *(Still seething)* Why, for God's sake?

CLARK Because you is a *Southren* boy. I is Southren too. Born and reared in Bolivar, Tennessee. Us Southren boys got to stick together. Born together. Die together. Dat's *equality*.

MAGRUDER   It's a pile of crap, if you want to know the truth, Lorenzo. Why do you hate Schwartz so much? Because he's Jewish?

CLARK   Because he a Jew-boy. *Yas!* An' because he afraid to believe he gwine to die. You an' me—us Southren boys —us *knows* we gwine die. Jew-boy, he gwine die too. He jus' skeered to own up to de nachel-born truth.

MAGRUDER   *(Angrily)*   What do you mean! He knows the truth. Schwartz is very sick. He's got advanced tuberculosis of the kidney. Every time he goes to the head, he pisses blood. He's *gravely ill* and he's terrified—like the rest of us. He doesn't want to die either. The only reason I can figure out why you hate him so is because he's Jewish. Why do you hate Jews like you do? Because they crucified Christ?

CLARK   No, man, because dey crucified de niggers. Ever hear tell of Ole Man Klein in my hometown of Bolivar, Tennessee? Mr. Samuel Klein who owned de Shoprite Department Sto'? My *daddy* owed Mr. Samuel Klein for ev'y blessed thing he had—owed fo' de raddio, 'frigerator, ten-piece suit of furniture in de front room, an' a fo'-foot picture of de Last Supper dat shined like de rainbow. Den dat year de cotton crop failed, and Daddy couldn't pay de 'stallments, and Mr. Samuel Klein he done *reclaim* ev'y stick, an' lef' dat house picked clean as a bone. *(Pauses)* Dat is de Jew *way!* Dat is de Jew way of skinnin' de black man's hide.

   (He falls back exhausted)

MAGRUDER   But listen, Lorenzo, it's not just the Jews who've skinned the niggers, it's been *everyone!* I mean, sure, I believe your story about this man Klein, but what about the other white people? What *they've* done to colored people! I mean the Presbyterians, the Methodists, the Baptists—

LINEWEAVER *(Enters, sleepy-looking and somewhat disheveled, from stage right, picking up on* MAGRUDER*'s last line in a singsong litany)* The Congregationalists, the Episcopalians, the Mormons, the Moravians, the Seventh Day Adventists—well, what *are* you two doing up so early, deep in your metaphysics? *(Loudly, to the ward at large)* All right, you gyrenes, first call! Out of those sacks in five minutes!

(The patients begin to groan and stir)

MAGRUDER *(There is an edge of compassion in his voice, as if he is trying to cope with or understand the irrationality of this Negro)* Can't you see how wrong and stupid it is of you to feel this way? It's a tough spot we're all in here. We're all in a terrible situation. Why don't you try to like Schwartz too, Lorenzo? It won't do any of us any good if you keep on storing up this unreasonable hatred. Hatred for someone who's done you not the slightest bit of harm.

CLARK *(Feebly but with passion)* I'll like de Jew boy. I *will* like him! I'll like him on de day dat de Lawd makes roses bloom in a pig's asshole.

*(*MAGRUDER *makes a silent gesture of hopelessness and disgust)*

LINEWEAVER *(Intercepts* SCHWARTZ *with a book, which the latter tries at first to conceal, then decides to bluff it out)* Good morning, Schwartz! You look chipper today. *(Puts his hand on* SCHWARTZ*'s brow)* Fever down a little. Good. Stick out the old tongue. *(Inspects his tongue)* Beautiful tongue. What are you doing up so early?

SCHWARTZ   I couldn't sleep. I went into the head to read my book.

LINEWEAVER *(Merely curious)*   Yeah? What are you reading these days?

SCHWARTZ   It's a Jewish book. It's called *Mazeltov*. It's a kind of a Jewish cookbook.

LINEWEAVER *(Amiably pats* SCHWARTZ *'s arm and moves off to his desk, stage left)*   Getting pretty fed up with the chow, huh, Schwartz? Well, I don't blame you. The food they give you guys I wouldn't feed to Captain Budwinkle.
(Winces slightly with his daring little jest. He then picks up some papers and charts from his desk and exits stage left. Now as the patients slowly rouse themselves, MAGRUDER *and* SCHWARTZ *sit on their adjacent beds and consult the book which has been appropriated)*

SCHWARTZ   Look, it's the biggest book I could find on syphilis. Also, it's got the longest title.

MAGRUDER   What's it called?

SCHWARTZ   *"The Complete Diagnostic and Therapeutic Source Book on Syphilis: A Guide to the Detection and Treatment of Syphilis, Acquired and Congenital; including Early Syphilis, both Primary and Secondary; Latent Syphilis, Early and Late; Late Syphilis; Cardiovascular Syphilis; Neurosyphilis; Meningovascular Syphilis; Locomotor Ataxia; and General Paresis.* Compiled by Martin J. McAfee, M.D., Isador Davidoff, M.D., Charles P. Dixon—"

MAGRUDER   Never mind who wrote it, Schwartz. What does it say? Especially what does it say about paresis? And locomotor ataxia? Those are two things I want to know most about.

SCHWARTZ *(An air of strained good humor in his voice)* Oh, I've got good news for you about them, Wally. Very good news indeed! *(Leafs through the index)* I would think things look very optimistic.

MAGRUDER Optimistic? How do you mean?

SCHWARTZ *(Refers to the book)* Well, get this—under "Locomotor Ataxia." In the part that talks about the prognosis. Get this. It says: "In about fifty percent of cases the disease becomes *stationary;* in the rest it progresses." There! Doesn't that make you optimistic?

MAGRUDER *(Reflects)* No, for God's sake! Why *should* it make me optimistic?

SCHWARTZ At least you've got a fifty-fifty chance of it not getting any worse.

MAGRUDER Oh, Jesus, yes, Schwartz, that makes me happy. Delirious! Why don't we break open a bottle of champagne? *(Puts his head in his hands)* Tell me some more.

SCHWARTZ Another very good piece of news. Listen. "Early, vigorous treatment improves the prognosis." There, that should make you feel better!

MAGRUDER *(Looks up)* But that's just the *point,* don't you see? How in God's name do I know—with me—if it's early? Like Dr. Glanz said, it may be already too *late.*

SCHWARTZ Well, that is true, Wally. That's something I suppose you just have to face. A fifty-fifty chance, though —it's not too bad. Not bad at all.

MAGRUDER O.K., let's say that I get all the symptoms tomorrow, but I'm lucky and it becomes stationary and doesn't progress. Tell me the good news.

SCHWARTZ *(Afraid of the dire revelation, hesitates)* Oh, Wally—

MAGRUDER Read it, Schwartz, damn it! I'm not afraid to know. Go ahead! Read! What *happens* when I get locomotor ataxia?

SCHWARTZ *(Reads with reluctant slowness)* "Inability to move in the dark or to maintain equilibrium with the eyes shut —Romberg's sign—is noticed. Walking becomes unsteady, and the characteristic staggering gait appears. The patient walks with legs apart, head bent forward, eyes fixed on the ground. Leg movements are excessive, the foot being thrown out high and the heel coming down sharply in a slapping gait." *(As* SCHWARTZ *reads,* MAGRUDER *compulsively and with a fanatical glint in his eye begins to ape these symptoms, rising and duplicating the leg and foot movements in the space between the beds)* "Sudden stopping or quick turning causes staggering and sometimes a fall. Canes are necessary until all locomotion becomes impossible—at which point the patient often lapses into other manifestations such as incontinence, blindness, impotence and paralysis."

MAGRUDER *(Ceases his pantomime and sinks onto the edge of the bed)* Christ on a fucking crutch!

SCHWARTZ Get this, though, Wally! It then says this: "Locomotor ataxia itself almost never causes death." Did you hear that? "Almost never causes death." Then *this:* "Many patients have lived twenty or twenty-five years or even longer."

MAGRUDER Twenty-five years in bed—pissing in my pajamas, paralyzed, impotent and blind.
     (He and SCHWARTZ *stare wordlessly at each other as* LINEWEAVER *enters at stage left)*

LINEWEAVER *(Strides across the ward)* Last call, boys! Drop your cocks and grab your socks! Hit the deck! Up and at 'em, gyrenes! Big treat in the mess hall this morning! Your choice of Post Toasties, Rice Krispies, or Wheaties, the Breakfast of Champions! Short-arm inspection in *precisely* ten minutes! *(Turns to DADARIO)* I'm going to miss you, Dadario. I'm going to miss the thrill of seeing that sensational tool of yours every day in the rosy dawn.
  (DADARIO, alone among the others this morning, has donned the khaki uniform of a marine private, and is preparing to leave with his sea-bag)

DADARIO I'm goin' to miss you too, Lineweaver. You've been just a darling through it all.

LINEWEAVER *(To the patients)* Say goodbye to Dadario, guys! Say farewell to a free man! *(A handful of the patients bid him goodbye in their various fashions. He then moves to the door, stage left, grinning, making a "V" for victory sign. LINE-WEAVER again addresses the ward at large)* There he goes, lads. Fit as a fiddle! Walking testimonial to the miracle of the healing sciences, of the triumph of Hygeia over the accursed gonococcus. As Dadario goes, so, in the fruition of time, shall ye all go!

MAGRUDER *(Watches DADARIO and LINEWEAVER exit, the latter going into the office to consult with DR. GLANZ, who has just arrived)* I wish there was some way I was able to believe that. *(Turns back to SCHWARTZ)* What's the book say about paresis, Schwartz? That's the one that really bothers me. Paralysis, to go blind—that's all bad enough, but *insanity*—
  (He breaks off with a shudder)

SCHWARTZ Very good news about paresis, Wally! Excellent news! *(Pauses, struggling to maintain his dauntless opti-*

mism) Maybe not so good news as with locomotor, but it still gives room for plenty of hope.

MAGRUDER   Like what?

SCHWARTZ   Well, listen. "Infrequently, remissions may occur to the extent of the patient being able to resume his occupation." There, how about that? You may get a remission. That's almost the same as being cured.

MAGRUDER   But didn't it say "infrequently"?

SCHWARTZ   Yes, it did.

MAGRUDER   Don't you know what infrequently means?

SCHWARTZ   Sure. Not frequent.

MAGRUDER   You think that's good news, then?

SCHWARTZ   Well, Wally, it's better than "never."

MAGRUDER *(Groans)*   What does it say about the symptoms?

SCHWARTZ *(Again hesitant)*   Wally, *Wally!* What's the point in all this? It's so painful. It's like picking at sores—

MAGRUDER   Go ahead and read it, Schwartz. Please! I'd rather know than not know.

SCHWARTZ *(Begins to read)*   "Most often the initial mental symptoms consist of insidious changes in personality, such as cleanliness of clothing and body." (SCHWARTZ *glances at* MAGRUDER, *who rather nervously straightens his robe, smooths back his hair, and in an abstracted way begins to clean his nails)* "Delusions concerning his property, position, family, or personal attainments may appear. A common first sign is the patient's suspicion that people in general are intent upon stealing his money or other belongings. On the other hand, with boastfulness and grandiosity he may believe himself a potentate or deity, the possessor of priceless jewelry, beautiful women, and fabulous wealth." *(Pauses and looks up)* I've never heard you boast about things like that, Wally. *(Half to himself)* Well, except maybe that girl— Anyway, you never talked like a potentate.

MAGRUDER *(Intensely nervous now)*   Not yet. Go on.

SCHWARTZ   "Serious defects in speech develop. In particular the consonants 'l' and 'r' are difficult for the paretic to enunciate. Hence he cannot readily articulate such test phrases as 'truly rural' . . . 'thirty-third artillery brigade' . . . 'around the rough and rugged rocks the ragged rascal ran' . . . and 'Methodist Episcopal.' "

LINEWEAVER *(Enters from GLANZ's office and strides briskly across the ward)*   Okey dokey, guys, VD patients fall out for *short-arm inspection! (As the patients slowly assemble at the foot of their beds, he approaches MAGRUDER)* Magruder, Dr. Glanz wants to see you at eleven o'clock—to start your sexual profile. *(With abrupt sympathy)* He's got the results of yesterday's blood test on you. Your Wassermann has risen from a three positive to a four positive. Incredible! That's as positive as you can get. *(Honestly commiserating)* I'm sorry, sonny boy. I'm really sorry about that. It's soared clean out of sight. *(Turns back and goes to GLANZ's office door)* VD patients all assembled for short-arm, sir!

GLANZ   Thank you, Lineweaver.

MAGRUDER *(Standing in a trance of anxiety now, gazing at SCHWARTZ)*   Each second, each minute, each hour: how they must be multiplying, those miserable little corkscrews! *(Pauses, then bursts out in a rage)* If I could *fight* this! If I could only *see* the enemy, I'd feel that I had a chance! But the little fuckers are deep inside me, burrowing away like a horde of hideous, microscopic *rats* and I can't get at them! *(Pauses)* And you know something else, Schwartz? You know what I feel? What I fear?

SCHWARTZ   What's that?

MAGRUDER   *Nothing's* going to get at them. No medicine! No cure! I'm going to end up a gibbering lunatic, scream-ing like a banshee in a padded cell. I can already *feel* those interminable days and nights—the horror!—my tongue no more able to grapple with speech than the tongue of a newborn baby. *(Pauses)* What are those words again, Schwartz?

SCHWARTZ   *(Reading)*   Let's see. Yes. "Truly rural."

MAGRUDER   *(Repeating the words, at first slowly, but then quickly and frantically)*   Truly rural . . . Truly rural.

SCHWARTZ   "Thirty-third artillery brigade."

MAGRUDER   Thirty-third artillery brigade!

SCHWARTZ   "Around the rough and rugged rocks the ragged rascal ran."

MAGRUDER   Around the rough and rugged rocks the ragged rascal ran!

SCHWARTZ   "Methodist Episcopal . . ."
        (The lights fade on the scene)

It is eleven o'clock the same morning. The scene is DR. GLANZ*'s office.* MAGRUDER *stands at stiff attention outside the office while* DR. GLANZ *explains the workings of a machine that sits on the desk to* CAPTAIN BUDWINKLE.

GLANZ   This is a remarkable new gadget for recording the human voice, sir. It has been distributed to a few select specialists. It's called a wire recorder.

BUDWINKLE   *(With great interest)*   Oh, yes, I've heard about them.

GLANZ   Warfare is an amazing human activity, sir. On the negative side, it does spawn social diseases such as the one that has afflicted our misguided young patient outside. *(Nods toward* MAGRUDER*)* But on the positive end of the scale, the technological end, the benefits must be incalculable. Think of the possibilities, in the postwar years, when a machine like this is simplified and refined, as it surely will be. Think of the ease with which we will be able imperishably to record the first cry of one's little pink baby, or a presidential speech, or several hours of uninterrupted inspiration from Dr. Norman Vincent Peale.

BUDWINKLE   Outstanding! Ace of an idea! Tell me though, Dr. Glanz, how is this machine applied in a practical sense to venereal patients?

GLANZ   As you well know, sir, most venereal patients are inveterate liars, and the machine helps bend them in the direction of the truth. A patient will choose his words more carefully if he knows that his statements are subject to scrutiny ex post facto.

BUDWINKLE   Fascinating. What is your technique of interrogation?

GLANZ   You will begin to see in a moment, sir, with our young syphilitic, Magruder. Today we start in with the first of two phases. This phase we call the Overview.

BUDWINKLE   The Overwhat?

GLANZ   The Overview, sir. The Grand Design. The motivational, the behavioral, the biosociological aspects of a patient's sexual profile. It is only after dealing in the more abstract that we can get to the more specific, the second phase. This we call the Blitz phase. In the Blitz phase—if you'll permit us a small witticism, sir—we come to the real *crotch* of the matter. But first, today, the Overview. Magruder, come in and be seated! (MAGRUDER *enters the office and takes a seat opposite* GLANZ *and* BUDWINKLE) We assume that Lineweaver has told you the state of your Wassermann, boy.

MAGRUDER   Yes, sir.
        (GLANZ *turns on the recorder*)

GLANZ   It means that you are extremely virulent. Therefore you must take the utmost pains to be truthful with us while we record your history on this machine. If you do so meticulously, we may be able to try to save your life. Do you understand?

MAGRUDER   Yes, sir.

GLANZ *(Consults some notes)*   First, it is our recollection that
you told us that you have had sexual congress with only
quote two women unquote in quote my entire life unquote, these females being quote an older woman unquote and quote my girl unquote. Is this correct?

MAGRUDER   I think so, sir.

GLANZ   What do you mean, "I think so"?

MAGRUDER   I got lost in all those quotes. I mean—yes, sir,
that's all correct.

GLANZ   Very well, what we want to know now is this. With
whom did you have relations *first*—the older woman or
the girl?

MAGRUDER   My girl, sir.

GLANZ *(Patiently)*   Now, Magruder, we don't mean for you
to describe the actual *carnal connection* with this girl. That
won't be necessary—at least for the moment. What we
want you to do is to outline your early relationship with
her, and the events leading up to the initial act of—coi-
tion. Tell us what it was that brought the two of you
together in the first place. We assume it was some powerful erotic attraction.

MAGRUDER   No, sir. It was poetry.

GLANZ   Poetry?

MAGRUDER   Well, we certainly had a powerful erotic attraction for each other. But that wasn't really the important
thing at all—not at first, at least. Like I say, it was poetry.
The other came later.

GLANZ   Kindly explain.
    (He fiddles with the machine)

6 1

MAGRUDER   In high school we had this senior English class together, Ann—that's her name—and I. Well, we just fell into reading a lot of poetry together, out loud.

BUDWINKLE   What *kind* of poetry? *Porno* poetry? Of the Whitman ilk?

MAGRUDER   Well, sir, as a matter of fact—yes. Funny you said that, sir. Walt Whitman and Shakespeare and Keats and—

BUDWINKLE   *(Interrupting)* Shakespeare, Whitman and Keats. Three fat English faggots. That's a *fine* gaggle of fruitimatoots to inspire manliness in a man.

MAGRUDER   Whitman's an American, sir.

BUDWINKLE   Never mind, they're all faggots. In England everybody's queer. Even the *strawberries* are queer in England. Only one English poet escaped being a pederast, and that was Kipling. *(Recites in an orotund voice)* "Now these are the Laws of the Jungle / and many and mighty are they / But the head and the hoof of the Law / and the haunch and the hump / is—*Obey!*" If you had been exposed to more poetry like that, Magruder, you might not be in your present pickle.

GLANZ   Well said, sir. Continue, Magruder.

MAGRUDER   Well, sir, I guess it was one of those weekends we'd been reading poetry together—one Saturday afternoon it was. There'd been a rainstorm, and my girl and I—we'd had to run across some fields and hole up in an old broken-down tobacco barn . . . and it was on that afternoon that I realized that I was in love with her. And I guess I knew she was in love with me. It was the first time for me, the first time I had made love to anyone, and somehow it was all mixed up with this poetry we'd discovered together. I imagine you could say it was like a religious experience—

BUDWINKLE *(Interrupts)* I imagine *you* could say it was like a religious experience, young friend. Most Americans do not equate divine worship with the act of fornication.

GLANZ That's very nice, Magruder, very idyllic. Very religious. But from our viewpoint you've left out an important detail. *(Pauses)* At this time, was the girl a virgin?

MAGRUDER Oh, yes, sir. I'm positive she was.

GLANZ Very well. I can only take your word. This, then, was the beginning of an affair during which, by your own admission, you had physical relations quote many, many times unquote. What we now want to know is this: How long did this affair last?

MAGRUDER Well, sir, it's still going on, I guess you could say. But it *was* interrupted.

GLANZ Kindly explain.

MAGRUDER I went with Ann all through the next year, until the beginning of the following summer. Then she had to go away. Her parents went away for the summer, to the beach, and took Ann with them.

GLANZ And you were alone. *(Pauses)* Alone. Deprived of your customary means of sexual release.

MAGRUDER *(Darkly)* Well, in a manner of speaking, sir. If you want to put it that way.

GLANZ Are we correct in assuming, then, that it was sometime during this summer that you encountered the "older woman" you mentioned, with whom you had the heretofore-mentioned sexual relations?

MAGRUDER   That's right, sir.

GLANZ   Kindly describe those relations in detail—

BUDWINKLE *(Interrupting)* Just a minute, Doctor. *(To* MA-
GRUDER*)* From all you have said, I take it you were very
much in love with this girl of yours. Right?
(He leans forward accusingly)

MAGRUDER   Yes, sir. Oh, yes, sir.

BUDWINKLE   I may be dense, Magruder. Obtuse. Stupid
even. Feel free to correct me if I don't make sense. But
one of the important aspects of love between man and
woman is *fidelity,* is it not? Decks clean fore and aft, and
all squared away amidships? *(Pauses)* I won't blow the
whistle on you for having premarital relations, although
that to my mind is a poisonous business. What I truly
can't abide—and I want you to hear it loud and clear—
is the idea that you betrayed this girl during her summer
vacation!
*(He leans back in his chair, folds his arms with a look of
consummate indignation)*

MAGRUDER *(Smarting badly under this assault, he nonetheless
begins to protest)* But, sir, if you'll let me try to explain—

GLANZ *(Severely)* Then explain, Magruder! In detail!

MAGRUDER   That summer there wasn't much to do at night,
and every now and then this friend of mine—his name
was Roy Davis—he and I would get some beer and drive
out in his father's car to this graveyard where it was quiet
and dark, and we'd sit and talk. One night we were sitting
there in the dark drinking beer, when this car came up
next to us. There were a couple of older women in the car
—it had been raining, but now the moon was out and we

could see them in the moonlight—and they were laughing and drinking beer too. They were pretty drunk, really. Roy and I said hello and they said hello back, and we all laughed a lot, and pretty soon they came over and got into our car. They'd just finished working the night shift at the cotton mill. Some people in my hometown look down on these cotton mill workers and call them lintheads.

GLANZ   Lintheads?

MAGRUDER   Yes, sir. They work around these looms and machines, and the lint from the cotton gets into their hair and makes it look fuzzy. That's why they're called lintheads.

GLANZ   These women are of a lower social class then, would you not say so? Lower than your own, which from your fact sheet would seem to be middle-middle-middle.

MAGRUDER   Yes, sir, I guess you could say that.

GLANZ   Their names? No, both names won't be necessary. Just the name of *your*—linthead.

MAGRUDER   That's a funny thing, sir. I never knew her complete name, her first name. But I did hear Roy's older woman say to my older woman something like "That husband of yours! That mean ole thing, Tom Yancey!" So ever since that night I've always remembered her as Mrs. Yancey.

GLANZ   *(Into microphone)*   Mrs. Thomas Yancey. *(To MA-GRUDER)* What else happened?

MAGRUDER   There's not a whole lot else to say, sir—except that we got horsing around in the car, the four of us, and

I'd drunk quite a bit of beer, and I guess you might say that—well, I was pretty *horny*. In fact, I was good and horny! And Mrs. Yancey, she was all over me. Playing with me and all. Boy, was *she* horny! She just wouldn't stop! And she kept kissing me and messing with me and messing with me and got me all excited, and I began to mess with her and she got pretty excited, too. *(Pauses)* So, sir, Mrs. Yancey and I just got out of the car and went into the graveyard and I—I had relations with her. On top of a tombstone.

GLANZ   On top of a tombstone? Ye gods!

MAGRUDER   Yes, sir, because the ground was real wet. So we chose one of those, you know, horizontal tombstones. I remember it was on top of somebody—I guess you could literally say some body—named McCorkle.

GLANZ   And you had one single connection with this woman. Why only once, when your past history indicates such—how shall we call it?—such vigorous erotic propensities?

MAGRUDER   Because Mrs. Yancey passed out, sir. And besides, it began to rain again.

GLANZ   *(Makes notes, shuffles papers, and regards* MAGRUDER *for a long moment with great solemnity)*   And so, Magruder, as the Captain has just implied, after this clammy encounter —this sordid little romp of yours—you soon returned to the embrace of your beloved, this girl, with perfect calm and equanimity. Had you *no* sense of guilt at all?

MAGRUDER   Well, sir, in a way I did. But I've thought over that night many times. *(A long pause)* I got awfully horny that night. And it was only once. I felt maybe Ann might have understood. She's pretty understanding.

GLANZ   Well, if you have no sense of guilt over this betrayal, perhaps you will be able to develop a sense of guilt over something far worse.

MAGRUDER   What's that, sir?

GLANZ   If, as you seem to have done, you took your girl's maidenhead, it would appear virtually impossible for her to have transmitted the disease to you. She would have been free from taint. So you obviously acquired your infection from this lower-class woman during your debauch that night in the cemetery. And the chances must be very close to one hundred percent that *you* in turn later transmitted the infection to this girl of yours.

MAGRUDER   But, sir—

GLANZ   No need to temporize, Magruder. The deed is done. Surely in the back of your *exceedingly* active mind there must have occurred that—that ugly probability.

MAGRUDER   *(Frantically)*   You mean—?

GLANZ   *(Emphatically)*   Yes. *(With a momentous pause)* That the disease that multiplies in you likewise multiplies *now* in that innocent, unsuspecting girl.

MAGRUDER   Oh, Jesus! *(Pauses) Maybe* in the back of my mind! But to have somebody—I mean a doctor, *you*—say it like this—*(Cries out)* But I've never meant to hurt anyone! *No one!* Least of all—*her!*

BUDWINKLE   Why are you crying, Magruder? For heaven's sake, stop it. *E-ech!* Crying in anyone over six makes my flesh crawl. Stop crying. I can't stand effeminacy.
   *(*MAGRUDER *continues to weep silently, chin propped in his palms, gazing with despair into space beyond his hands)*

GLANZ   Stop crying, Magruder, as the Captain commands
you! We insist you stop crying!

(*He and* BUDWINKLE *stand over* MAGRUDER *now, exhort-
ing him to cease crying, as he gazes into space, saying nothing, weeping helplessly. The scene ends in darkness, with
"We insist you stop crying!"*)

ACT THREE

Eugene Troobnick as SCHWARTZ, Nicholas Hormann as LINEWEAVER, Miles Chapin as MAGRUDER, Bill Ludel as MC DANIEL and Steven Robman as MARINE CORPORAL.

It is several days later, mid-morning. MAGRUDER *sits alone, writing a letter. On the part of the ward near stage left a blackjack game is in progress. The players are* STANCIK, McDANIEL *and another. Their laconic cardplayers' dialogue—"Hit me," "I'll stick," "Hit me hard," etc.—is the first sound heard.* SCHWARTZ *is absent, while* CLARK *lies in his bed, with customary balefulness silently surveying the scene. In* DR. GLANZ's *office,* LINEWEAVER *stands awaiting instructions from the doctor, who is seated at his desk.* MAGRUDER *puts his pen and paper down, rises and goes toward the head, stage left. As he walks, he trips clumsily and obviously over a bedpan on the floor, then recovers himself, exiting stage left.*

GLANZ   He'll be free to go Monday. (*Hands* LINEWEAVER *an envelope*) That'll be all for the moment, Lineweaver.

LINEWEAVER   Aye-aye, sir. (*Turns and leaves the office, walks onto the ward and approaches the blackjack players*) Stancik, I got good news for you. (STANCIK *and the other two look up*) Your dingdong doesn't leak any more, your smears for gonococci were negative, your prostate is peachy, your vas deferens is a dream, your urethra is adorable, your epididymus won the gold medal at the epididymus show —and you get out of here on Monday. Here are your marching orders.

STANCIK (*Exuberant*)   I told you I'd win that bet, McDaniel! I told you I'd beat that bug and be out of here by next week! Give me my five bucks!

McDANIEL *(Turning up a card)* Twenty-one. Pay me. *(Casually)* I'll deduct it from your blackjack account, Stancik. You owe me two hundred and twenty thousand dollars. Minus five.

LINEWEAVER Congratulations, Stancik.

STANCIK *(Looks at his orders)* It's really true. I'm gonna get out! *(Gazes into space with an exultant look)* I can't wait for my first liberty. I'm gonna go to Norfolk. Oh, man, I'm gonna go to Norfolk and shack up with this broad I met—

LINEWEAVER *(Interrupts)* I hope you have an independent income, Stancik. Because on account of the clap, and on account of how long it took to cure you, I calculate you've forfeited your pay until about five years from now. You'll be in hock for that spectacular dose of yours when the war's over and everybody else has gone home.

STANCIK Ah, Christ, I *forgot* about that!

LINEWEAVER As for talk about shacking up with any broad, Stancik, let me tell you, you're a real marvel, a *phenomenon.* You go against *Nature!* Ulcer patients can't bear to think about eating, guys with fallen arches shudder at the idea of having to walk, people with laryngitis—the *last* thing they want to do is to talk. Every patient I ever saw come on this ward gets so turned off sex you'd think they were eunuchs. But *you,* Stancik, you're incredible! I swear to God, I think you've been here since before the clap was discovered, yet day in and day out, rain or shine, with the ghastly wages of *venery* manifest on every hand, all I've ever heard you talk about is *ass.* I dunno, you're *stupefying,* a real tribute to the life force or something.
    (While he is talking, MAGRUDER *reenters from stage left and trips over the same bedpan)*

MAGRUDER *(In a desperate whisper)* Methodist Episcopal! *(He goes to his chair and sinks down heavily, head in his hands)*

LINEWEAVER *(Attention caught by* MAGRUDER, *he approaches him)* How you feeling, sonny boy?

MAGRUDER *(Despondently raises his head)* Yesterday's blood test? How was it?

LINEWEAVER Sorry, I wish I could bring you some cheer. But it's still holding the line right up there. *(Looks at him closely)* Are you really feeling all right? You look a bit feverish. *(Feels his brow)* Hmm. You're a little warm. I'll take your temperature in a minute. How are you feeling?

MAGRUDER Not very good, to be quite honest. All sort of achey and, you know, *blah*— And you know another thing? My gums have begun to bleed like crazy.

LINEWEAVER Open up. *(Inspects his gums)* Mmmh. Quite so. Rather inflamed.

MAGRUDER They're not bleeding now, but Jesus, whenever I brush my teeth—*(Halts, and there is a new edge of anxiety in his voice)* You don't really think that—I mean—*(Breaks off)* What do you think it means?

LINEWEAVER I dunno. I *just* don't know. We'd better have that checked out. *(He strides toward stage left, looking worried and preoccupied)* We'd just better have that checked out. *(He exits)*

CLARK *(Rises up on his elbow in bed, laughing his malicious little laugh)* It's dem *spiral*-keets. De *spiral*-keets, dey movin' right up. Dey in yo' mouf. Dat's how come you bleedin'. Dey movin' *right* up. Pretty soon dey gwine be *right* up yere. *(Grins as he points to his skull)* Den—dat's all! Tee-hee.

(MAGRUDER, *absorbing what* CLARK *says, glaring at him but ignoring him, sits down to write a letter. After a moment of writing, he suddenly crumples up the letter, hurls it across the ward, and rises in a rage*)

MAGRUDER (*Speaks in the direction of* CLARK, *but his anguish now is really voiced inward to himself*) Yet I'm lying to her! Not only am I a sack of corruption, I'm a shameless, unspeakable liar! All because I don't have the courage, the guts to tell her the *truth.* (*Pauses, his agony growing more intense*) But the *truth!* How can you tell that kind of truth? How can you tell someone that you've filled them with some evil pollution? Jesus, I've *got* to tell her, but how do you find words for such hideous news? (*Pauses*) And that Goddamned Mrs. Yancey! I'd write her too if I knew her address! I'd write her and tell her to stop cruising around graveyards and contaminating people!

CLARK (*Slowly, passively, distantly*) Dem *spiral*-keets. Dey is trouble. Dey is *baa-ad* trouble.

MAGRUDER (*Begins to write, tears up a sheet of paper, then repeats this action in despair. He then reaches into the pocket of his robe in search of his wallet, frantically pats the other pocket, finds the wallet gone*) My wallet! (*To* CLARK) My wallet! My wallet with her pictures! (*Begins to dig around in his seabag, looks under the mattress and under the bed*) My wallet! It's gone!

CLARK How much money you done had in dere, white boy?

MAGRUDER I don't know. Not much. (*His voice becomes distraught*) Not much! Five dollars, maybe six. But it's not the money. It's her pictures! Those snapshots of my girl. There were three of them. And they're gone!

CLARK *(Beckons to him)* Come here. I want tell you somethin'. *(His voice becomes conspiratorial as* MAGRUDER *approaches)* Listen close while I tells you somethin'.

MAGRUDER *(Wildly impatient)* What?

CLARK Somebody *took* dat wallet, and I seed it wid mah own eyes.

MAGRUDER Well *who,* then? *Who* took it?

CLARK De Jew-boy took it!

MAGRUDER *(Draws back, incredulous)* Schwartz? Schwartz took my wallet? You're crazy, Lorenzo! Crazy! Schwartz wouldn't steal anyone's wallet!

CLARK I'm *tellin'* you! Swear befo' God three times and hopes I goes straight to *hell* if'n dat Jew-boy didn't steal you' wallet. *(His voice, though enervated, is filled with passion and conviction)* It were *he!*

MAGRUDER *(Still incredulous, but weakening)* When did you see Schwartz steal my wallet, Lorenzo? Don't lie about this. I know you hate him, but don't accuse some innocent man!

CLARK He stole hit las' night. In de dead of night I seed him grab it. Awake all night I was, jest a-lyin' here with my eyes cracked open, and I seed de Jew-boy git up to go to de head. Den by an' by he come back, and he seed dat wallet in yo' robe hangin' dere, and he *tuk* it. He tuk it clean on out'n dat robe and carried it wid him to bed. Dat is a Jew thief!

MAGRUDER *(Weakening further)* I can't believe this. *(Pauses)* I just can't believe that somebody like Schwartz would steal anyone's wallet.
(He continues to search around his bed)

7 5

CLARK *(His voice intimate, confidential)* Hit well known. One thing. De Jew peoples *do* like money—

MAGRUDER *(Protesting)* Oh, come on, Lorenzo. That's an old, ridiculous—

CLARK *(Interrupting)* Let me ax you somethin'! Who else dey *is* to steal it but de Jew-boy? *(Gestures to the three beds)* Dere *you* is. Dere *he* is. Here *I* is. An' *I*—I can't move any inch. We de only ones dis end ob de hospital. So ain't no one but de Jew-boy *could* steal it. Hee-hee! Less'n you gone steal it yo'self.

MAGRUDER *(Pauses, deeply perplexed, but beginning to see some logic in this)* But I just can't accept the idea that someone like Schwartz—

CLARK *(Interrupts again, angrily)* I doesn't *lie*, white boy. Enough! Believe me or believe me not! I don't keer!
        (CLARK rolls over weakly. During his last speech, SCHWARTZ has appeared at stage left. As CLARK rolls over, SCHWARTZ moves across the ward toward MAGRUDER. Walking, he displays a new quality of debilitation, exemplified in a certain slow, halting feebleness of gait)

SCHWARTZ Hello, Wally. How you feelin', Wally?

MAGRUDER *(With a certain stiffness and coolness)* Not so good, thank you.

SCHWARTZ *(In an offhand way, devoid of self-pity, as he fumbles for something in his seabag)* Well, with me it's very much the same as you. I had another examination this morning. You know these pains I began to have the other night? *(Looks fearfully up at MAGRUDER)* They think my condition has spread now. Spread. *(Pauses)* Spreading!

MAGRUDER *(Cool, stiffly polite)* Schwartz, I've got to ask you something.

SCHWARTZ Certainly, Wally. What is it?

MAGRUDER Have you seen my wallet? It's missing.

SCHWARTZ Your wallet? You mean, have I ever seen your wallet? Why, yes, I saw it the other day. When you were looking at those pictures of your girl.

MAGRUDER No, not *then*. I mean since last night.

SCHWARTZ No, Wally, I honestly can't say that I have.

MAGRUDER Schwartz, I hate to— I've got to ask you something. Did you take my wallet?

SCHWARTZ *(So dumbfounded that he can barely speak for a moment)* Did I steal your wallet? *Did I steal your wallet!*

MAGRUDER *(Wildly agitated now)* Not steal! I said *take!* I'm not accusing you of stealing it. Only taking it. Taking it, see? Taking it maybe because you wanted to borrow five dollars to go to the PX this morning and didn't want to wake me up to ask for it. Something like that. I'm not accusing you of *stealing* it, only taking it. But now I want it back! Where is it, Schwartz? I want that wallet back!

SCHWARTZ *(In anguish)* No! I didn't *touch* your wallet! What are you saying? I've never stolen a thing in my life. *(He advances resentfully on MAGRUDER, pressing close)* Except for that fuckin' *book*, which I stole *for you!*

MAGRUDER *(Edging away but still furious)* Quit breathing on me. Admit you *stole* that wallet!

SCHWARTZ I'm *not* breathing on you. *(Coming even closer)* And I didn't steal your fuckin' wallet! Only somebody like *you*—some dirty, degenerate *Southern-born cracker* would accuse an innocent man of something like that! *(They advance on each other, fists clenched)*

CLARK *(Suddenly interrupting)* Hey, Jew-boy! *Tolerance!* Hee-hee!
(On this last outburst, LINEWEAVER *has entered from stage left, and immediately rushes to break up the fracas)*

LINEWEAVER Break it up! Break it up! What's going on here? No fighting among the invalids. Dr. Glanz's orders. *(He interposes himself between the two, gently pushing* MAGRUDER *back and away)* Interesting idea, though. The first matched bout between syphilis and consumption. *(Adds to* MAGRUDER, *almost as an afterthought)* Take it easy, sonny boy. Oh, they found this wallet of yours at the hospital laundry. *(Hands him the wallet)* It was in your other robe. There's some honesty left, even in the U.S. Navy.
(He exits stage right. There is a long silence, pregnant with a sense of humiliation)

MAGRUDER You've got to forgive me, Schwartz. How can I ever apologize for saying what I said to you just now? *(Turns toward* CLARK's *bed)* And you! You, Lorenzo. You're a black no-good nigger son of a bitch.

CLARK Hee-hee!

SCHWARTZ *(Sitting down weakly)* Don't, Wally! It's no use calling him names. I should have known that he was at the bottom of it all. I had forgotten what he was capable of. *(Turns to* CLARK*)* But, oh, Clark, you're an evil *schwarze.* I've never known anyone as evil as you.

CLARK Hee-hee!

SCHWARTZ   Clark!

CLARK   What do you want, Jew-boy?

SCHWARTZ   *(At white heat)*   Hey, listen, Clark, why can't you ever once call me by my real name? I mean, that's not so much to ask, is it? I call you by *your* real name. I don't call you nigger. I call you *Clark*, you nigger! *(CLARK laughs)* Oh, boy, Clark, if there ever lived a nigger who deserved to be called a nigger, you, Clark, are that nigger, you *nigger!*

CLARK   Jew-boy don' like to be called a Jew-boy, 'cause de Jew-boy *is* a Jew-boy, and who wants to be a Jew-boy?

MAGRUDER   I'm sorry about it all, Schwartz. Sorry from the bottom of my heart. I hope you'll accept my apology.

SCHWARTZ   You don't have to apologize, Wally. I understand. I'm sorry too for what *I* said. *(Pauses and gazes about him, as if to emphasize, silently, his hatred and fear of the place)* When—when you accused me just now, I could only think all of a sudden, "It's his sickness that's making him do that." I said to myself, "Remember? That's all part of his sickness."

MAGRUDER   *(With dawning apprehension)*   What do you mean? What do you mean, Schwartz—all part of my sickness?

SCHWARTZ   Nothing, Wally.

MAGRUDER   *(With great anxiety)*   Tell me what you meant by that!

SCHWARTZ   *(Placatingly)*   Really nothing, Wally. Nothing. Nothing at all.

MAGRUDER   You mean about the money? And what it said in that book?

SCHWARTZ *(Reluctantly)* Well, yes—

MAGRUDER What did the book say?

SCHWARTZ Wally, Wally, don't *torment* yourself.

MAGRUDER But what did it say? *You* remember.

SCHWARTZ It said something like, When you've got paresis, one of the first signs is the patient's suspicion that other people are intent on stealing from him.

MAGRUDER *(Sits down slowly, with a stunned and frightened look)* My God, yes. I'd forgotten that. Oh, my God! *(Turns to* CLARK*)* But I had good cause! I mean, Lorenzo there—he was behind it all. *(Pauses)* Even so! I wouldn't have said that to you if I wasn't sick! *(Pauses again with a look of terror, then thrusts his hands against his forehead)* Like Dr. Glanz said, it's gone to my brain! I'm mad! Stark raving mad! Stark raving mad! Stark raving mad! Stark raving mad!

> *(Pandemonium erupts. He goes into a delirium, and has to be controlled and placated. The lights fade)*

It is several days later, mid-morning. MAGRUDER *is absent.* CLARK *is absent too, his bed freshly made-up and empty.* SCHWARTZ *is in bed for the first time, lying with a thermometer in his mouth as he reads his book* How to Manage a Pet Shop. *As the scene opens,* LINEWEAVER *strides across the ward from stage left and stops at* SCHWARTZ*'s bed to examine the thermometer.*

LINEWEAVER   Hmm. Not bad. How do you feel this morning, old pal?

SCHWARTZ *(Strokes his abdominal area)*   The pain's not there so much now. Not like last night. That was terrible!

LINEWEAVER   Did that shot I gave you help any?

SCHWARTZ   Oh, yes, I went fast asleep. It took the pain right away. And, you know, I had these wonderful dreams. Fantastic dreams! Dreams filled with all sorts of animals. Funny, it must come from reading my book here, about running a pet shop.

LINEWEAVER *(Feeling* SCHWARTZ*'s pulse)*   That's good. Good to have the pain go away and dream nice dreams.

SCHWARTZ   In one of them I dreamed I was in this pet shop I'm going to buy after the war's over. Only it's strange, you know, there weren't any cages. The animals—they were all running around free. *(Pauses)* What a funny dream. Anyone knows you can't have a pet shop without cages.

LINEWEAVER *(Abstractedly)* Mmm-hmm. Strange thing about dreams. What's your pleasure, Schwartz? You'd like some orange juice? How about some orange juice with a lot of crushed ice?

SCHWARTZ Yeah, that might be nice.

LINEWEAVER *(Moves away)* I'll have it sent up from the galley. *(At extreme stage left he encounters ANDERSON, one of the hospital corpsmen, and speaks to him out of SCHWARTZ's hearing. To indicate the gravity of SCHWARTZ's condition, he makes a series of nervous jabbing downward motions with his thumb)* I don't know if that morphine has worn off or not. If he begins to hurt again, give him eight more milligrams I.V.

> *(He exits. For a moment SCHWARTZ continues to read, then MAGRUDER enters stage right, carrying his seabag. He still wears the robe with its embroidered "S")*

MAGRUDER Hi, Schwartz.

SCHWARTZ *(Looking up)* Wally! Welcome back! I thought you were gone for good.

MAGRUDER No, Schwartz, no such luck. It was my gums. Remember how my gums were bleeding? They put me upstairs on the observation ward for four days and gave me a lot of dental treatment. Guess what they found out? *(Pauses)* Trench mouth. I had trench mouth.

SCHWARTZ So now you're back.

MAGRUDER So now I'm back.

SCHWARTZ Back.

MAGRUDER Back. *(Long pause)* Anyway, they cured my trench mouth. They put some purple medicine on my gums that made me look like a Ubangi, and it cleared up in forty-eight hours. *(Pauses)* Wonderful, pure mouth I've got now. Clean and trouble-free. A mouth any girl would love to kiss. If she didn't know what else I had. *(Pauses again, looks around)* Where's Lorenzo?

SCHWARTZ Clark? *(Silence for a moment)* He's dead.

MAGRUDER *Dead? (Another silence)* I can't believe it! Jesus!

SCHWARTZ He went fast, Wally. How long have you been gone? Four days? He must have—died on Tuesday, the second day after you left. Just after you went upstairs he fell into this kind of stupor, I guess you'd call it. Dr. Glanz and Lineweaver and everybody tried to bring him around, but it was no use. *(Pauses)* Boy, did he smell bad toward the end!

MAGRUDER *(Brooding)* It's sad. Hateful as he was, it's sad. I guess it always is. *(Pauses)* It's hard to believe. Lorenzo's dead.

SCHWARTZ It *was* sad. I couldn't help feeling terribly sorry for him when he went into that stupor—even after all the ugly and vicious things he's said. *(Pauses)* You know, Wally, I felt so sorry for him that I had to try to communicate with him. His face turned kind of blue—a strange deep kind of blue like ink welling up through his black skin—and his lips curled back from his teeth in this awful look of agony. It wrenched something out of me—out of my heart. He seemed so alone in his dying. So helpless.

MAGRUDER Did you say anything to him? Did you get *to* him somehow?

SCHWARTZ In a way, I guess you'd say. But not really, even though I tried. I don't know, Wally, as I got up and looked at him, looking at that fuckin' agony on his face, and watching him breathe in this tortured way, I said to my-self, "Well, he's dying." And so I looked in Rabbi Wein-

berg's book, in the index, under D for Death. And I read
Lorenzo that wonderful line that goes like this: "Dying
is a beautiful and natural part of the life process, no more
to be feared than sleep." And I heard Lorenzo say, very
softly: "Dat is mule shit." Then I said to myself, "This
hatred of his, it's only because of the hatred that we in
turn—we whose skins are white—have poured out on
him. I thought I should ask Lorenzo to forgive me—to
forgive us—for all we've done to him, so I looked in the
book under Forgiveness and read that fantastic thought
that goes: "The most noble of human gifts is the gift of
forgiveness." And then I said, "Don't you understand,
Lorenzo? Can't you forgive me?" And his voice was so
terribly weak and faint. I heard him say, "Forgiveness."
And he gave that funny little laugh and said again, "Forgiveness. Dat do grab my black ass." *(Pauses)* Wally,
Wally, I was desperate! He was fading there, dying right
in front of my eyes. I felt that I just *couldn't* let him go
with this hatred all bottled up inside him. Somehow I just
had to reach him with the message of brotherhood. So I
read that passage in the book where the Rabbi quotes
from Beethoven's Ninth Symphony *"Alle Menschen werden
Bruder"*—I hope I'm pronouncing it right—"All mankind become brothers when they join hands and love one
another." Then I stopped reading and I looked down at
him and said: "Lorenzo, we mustn't live and die with this
awful hate inside us. We must be brothers and love one
another." Then at last I said, "I love you, Lorenzo. I love
you as a brother. Please allow yourself to love me in
return." *(Pauses)* And finally he spoke—so faint and weak
—they must have been almost the last words he said. And
you know what they were? *(Pauses)* He said, "Yes, I'll love
you. *(Pauses)* "*Yes*, I'll love you! I will love you, Jew-boy.
I will love you when the Lord makes roses bloom in a
pig's asshole."

(At this moment the light goes up in the office of DR. GLANZ, *who in pantomine begins to converse with* LINEWEAVER*)*

MAGRUDER *(After pondering* SCHWARTZ*'s words)* Well, he stuck by his guns to the end. You have to give him that. *(Pauses)* And you, Schwartz. How are things with you?

SCHWARTZ *(Makes a little "like-this-like-that" gesture with his hand)* Oh, I don't know, Wally, I've had better days. But it's good to see you. Even though I know you're not glad *you're* back.

MAGRUDER *(Mournfully)* No, Schwartz, I'm not glad I'm back.

SCHWARTZ *(Tentatively)* Had any—had any bad symptoms?

MAGRUDER No. *(Pauses)* Well, I don't know. I tripped again the other day, and I thought—locomotor ataxia! I was in a terrible sweat all that day, but it didn't come back. *(Pauses)* I don't know, Schwartz. By now I'm pretty well resigned to whatever's got to come.

SCHWARTZ You look *fine*, Wally. I wouldn't worry about a stumble like that. Your legs are all wobbly from too little exercise, that's all. You really look fine. I wish I felt as healthy as you look.

MAGRUDER If I looked like I felt you'd see a syphilitic marine of a hundred and six.

SCHWARTZ *(In some pain now, he makes a small groan)* Aaah-h!

MAGRUDER What's wrong? Do you need—

SCHWARTZ It's nothing. It comes and goes, the pain. I'll be all right.

LINEWEAVER *(Enters from stage left, where he has been talking with* DR. GLANZ*)* Magruder, you're going to help Uncle

Sugar win the war after all. Both of the Wassermann tests you had on the observation ward were totally negative.

MAGRUDER *(Stupefied)*   What on earth are you talking about?

LINEWEAVER   It turns out you're clean as a whistle. You've got no more syphilis than Mickey Mouse.

MAGRUDER   I don't know what you mean!

LINEWEAVER   Your diagnosis has been changed to a false positive Wassermann due to trench mouth.

MAGRUDER   Some kind of joke. *(Bursts out in a rage)* No jokes, Lineweaver! None of your smartass jokes! I can't *take* anything like that, hear me!

LINEWEAVER *(Grasps him by the arms to calm him)*   It's not a joke, sonny boy! You'll live to die a hero on a wonderful Pacific beach somewhere. That's a lot better, isn't it, than ending up with the blind staggers, or in the booby hatch? And if you really die with enough dash and style, they might even give you the Navy Cross.

MAGRUDER *(Still stunned)*   But I don't understand!

LINEWEAVER   Simple. Let me explain. The Wassermann test is almost foolproof. In rare cases, however—once in thousands of times—some other disease will turn up a false reaction. Malaria is one, for instance. Trench mouth's another. When the dental surgeon cured your trench mouth, your Wassermann went negative—plop!— just like that.

MAGRUDER *(Breaking away from his grasp)*   What are you saying, Lineweaver? Do you realize what you're saying?

LINEWEAVER *(Cajolingly)*   I'd better let the boss man say the rest, sonny boy. Dr. Glanz'll explain. He wants to see you right now. Oh, by the way, here are your orders. You can report back to your outfit tomorrow.

(He hands him his orders)

MAGRUDER *(Still in a state of shock, wrestling with this new knowledge like a man reprieved from a death sentence, he walks dazedly to* DR. GLANZ *'s office)* Negative Wassermann? False Positive! *Trench mouth!*

> *(He pauses in front of* DR. GLANZ *'s door, and it is immediately apparent from his suddenly rigid stance that he is aware of what is going on within. At this point, our attention is caught by* DR. GLANZ, *who sits silently before the wire recorder in his office, in deep contemplation, listening to his own interview with* MAGRUDER; *the expression on his face is sensual, flushed, unabashedly erotic)*

GLANZ'S VOICE Blitz phase. Session number two. *(Pause)* Now, Magruder, we want to remind you again that you must describe your physical relations with the girl in your very own words, repeat, *your very own words.* Now then *(Pauses)*—Did the nipples of her breasts grow pink and excited when you stroked them with your hand?

MAGRUDER'S VOICE *(In a tone of protest)* Well, sir—*(Pauses)* Yes, sir, they *did,* but—

GLANZ'S VOICE *(Sternly)* In your own words, Magruder! We *insist* on your own words!

MAGRUDER'S VOICE Well, sir, then yes. The nipples of her breasts grew pink and excited when I stroked them with my hand.

> *(*GLANZ *stops the machine and plays back twice the last sentence above, then lets the machine run on)*

GLANZ'S VOICE And her thighs. Were they warm and smooth when you caressed them?

MAGRUDER'S VOICE Yes, sir, her thighs were warm and smooth when I caressed them.

(The recorder clicks off and MAGRUDER *enters the office, his fists clutched in fury)*

GLANZ *(Suddenly flustered)* The Scottish people have an ancient saying, our boy: "The best laid schemes of mice and man aft gang aglay." Do you know what that implies? Have you heard that saying?

MAGRUDER *(Slowly, trancelike, almost mesmerized, with the first seeds of rage being sown in his mind)* It's not an ancient saying. It's from a poem by Robert Burns. Sir. *(The "Sir" is added following a pause, almost as an afterthought)* And it's "gang aft aglay."

GLANZ At any rate, you may understand the implication. It is relevant, also, to our modern scientific marvels. The best-made instruments of medical research and diagnosis do, from time to time, gang slightly aglay. The Wassermann test is an example. Superb a tool as it is for detecting disease, it is not infallible. In your case, regrettably, it did prove fallible.

MAGRUDER *(His voice a tentative murmur)* Then why didn't you tell me—

GLANZ *(Not hearing his beginning protest)* As Lineweaver has doubtless told you, your positive reaction was caused by the latent trench mouth which you had when you took your first blood test and which erupted full-blown while you were here. The causative organisms—the spirochetes of trench mouth and syphilis—are quite similar. While this reaction rarely happens, it *does* happen—

MAGRUDER *(The voice still remote, but growing stronger)* You could have *told* me.

GLANZ What say, Magruder?

MAGRUDER *(Very loud now)* You could have—*told* me!

GLANZ *(Slightly rattled by his tone)* Told you what?

MAGRUDER *(His words very precise and measured in his rage, which is barely controlled now)* Told me what you just told me now.

GLANZ We don't quite understand—

MAGRUDER *(Frankly aggressive now, heedless of his subordinate position)* Then I'll try to *make* you understand. If what you say is true you could have given me some *hope.* You could have told me that I *might* have had some other disease. Latent trench mouth. Athlete's foot! Ringworm! Something else! Anything! You could have been less god-damned certain that I was going to *die* full of paresis and locomotor ataxia!

GLANZ *(Alarmed by MAGRUDER's tone, rises from his chair)* Mind your tone, Magruder. We're in authority here! The reason we failed to give you such information is because it is our firm policy never falsely to arouse a patient's expectations, his hopes—

MAGRUDER *(Fully exercised now, he advances in a fury on the doctor, circling the corner of his desk)* Hope! What do you know about hope and expectations! Don't talk to me about hope and expectations, you wretched son of a bitch!

GLANZ You're insubordinate, Magruder! You'll get a court-martial for this! You're speaking to a lieutenant commander in the United States Navy!

MAGRUDER *(Coming closer to GLANZ, who is now plainly frightened, he seizes a light metal chair and brandishes it at the doctor much as a lion tamer would)* Pipe down, you hear! *I'm* going to have something to say now. Don't give me any of the lieutenant-commander crap! To me you're some kind of terrible Gauleiter. The only difference between you and an SS man is that an SS man doesn't stink of chloroform. Give me that recording, you filthy sadistic pig!

GLANZ *(In a panic now)*   Magruder, you must have taken leave of your senses! Desist, we say! Leave off! *(In the direction of the door)* Corporal of the Guard! *(To* MAGRUDER*)* We protest this—this—

MAGRUDER *(Interrupting him, he drops the chair and pinions* GLANZ *to the wall by the neck)*   Don't give me any more of this "we" shit, either! You're not Congress, or some goddamned corporation, or the King of Sweden! You're a loathsome little functionary with a dirty mind and a stethoscope, and goddamn you, from now on I insist you say *I*—like niggers, Jews and syphilitics! Give me that recording!

GLANZ *(Trying desperately to appease him)*   Magruder, boy, stop! Let us explain. Ow! You're hurting us! Let us try to explain. Ow! Ow! You might fracture our hyoid bone!

MAGRUDER   *Me!* Not *us!* Say let *me* try to explain, dammit.

GLANZ *(Acquiescing in a choked voice)*   Let *me* try to explain. Ow! Ow! You're compressing our submaxillary gland!

MAGRUDER *(Still attacking, with his hands grasping the doctor's neck, he roughly shoves* GLANZ *down into his own chair)*   Start explaining!

GLANZ   First, we want to say—

MAGRUDER   "*I*" want to say—

GLANZ   First I want to ask you—

MAGRUDER   Hold it, Glanz! *I'm* going to ask the questions around here now. Listen again. Answer me. Tell me once more why it was you didn't let me know that there was a possibility—a *chance*, no matter how remote—of my being sick from something else.

GLANZ   Because, as I said, it has always been our—*my* policy never to falsely arouse a patient's hopes. Ow! You're hurting my trachea!

MAGRUDER   You lie, Glanz. It's because you got your jollies that way. That's the way you got your kicks!

GLANZ   That's unfair, Magruder! Unfair! I am a *healer*. I have taken the Hippocratic oath. It would have been cruel to arouse in you unfounded expectations—

MAGRUDER   (*Breaking in*)   You're not a healer, Glanz! You're a ghoul. You feed off the very dregs of death.

GLANZ   (*Struggling to get free again*)   That's a slander, a vile slander! As a dedicated urologist sworn to alleviate human suffering I resent these canards, these accusations—

MAGRUDER   (*Forcing him back down*)   Pipe down, you creep! There's just a little bit more for me to say, and to hear you say; then you can serve me up to your policemen, your brig apes. There's something else I want to know. These *profiles* of yours, those miserable . . . filthy . . . pornographic examinations. What about them, Glanz? What purpose did they serve, except to jerk off and titillate that dirty mind of yours? Oh, I want that recording. I want somebody else to hear you at your work!

GLANZ   (*Howls with chagrin*)   Unfair again, Magruder. Foul! A foul aspersion! Without a biography in depth such as I took of you I should never have properly located your disease as having emanated from that older woman . . . with . . . whom (*Begins to realize what he is saying, and his voice fades)* you . . . had . . . relations. *(Pauses)* I never would have . . . pinpointed . . . the . . . uh . . . *source* . . . *(Halts)* I mean, Magruder—

(*There is a prolonged silence now as they gaze at each other intently, the revelation in* GLANZ *'s words creating an unspoken understanding*)

It is the same day, several hours later. MAGRUDER *sits on the chair by his bed, writing a letter. Dressed in a khaki shirt and pants, he is guarded by a* MARINE CORPORAL, *with an MP brassard and billy club, who stands nearby.* LINEWEAVER *enters from stage left to examine* SCHWARTZ, *who lies listlessly in bed in a half-doze.*

LINEWEAVER How's everything, Schwartz?

SCHWARTZ *(After a pause)* Better, I think. Those shots— they work.

LINEWEAVER *(Pats his shoulder)* Good man. *(Turns away from* SCHWARTZ, *and approaching* MAGRUDER, *stands above him with his hands on his hips, addressing him rather like a parent to a wayward offspring)* Sonny boy, you got yourself into real trouble, didn't you? *(To the* MARINE CORPORAL*)* When do you take him to the brig?

MARINE CORPORAL Any time now, I guess. I've gotta wait for Captain Budwinkle to finish writing out his report on the prisoner.

LINEWEAVER Oh, you got yourself into *real* trouble, sonny boy. You might have committed murder or *sodomy*, or you might have run your ship aground on a reef—there are many terrible crimes in the naval service. But to have done what you did! To assault a superior officer! Oh, baby doll, the mind boggles at what they're going to do to you!

MAGRUDER *(Without emotion, and with exaggeratedly polite curiosity)* What's that, Lineweaver? What *are* they going to do?

LINEWEAVER Well, when a sailor or a marine does something truly bad they send him to a big prison up in Portsmouth, New Hampshire. I'm sure you've heard of it. For what you did there's a special place *underneath* that prison where they bury you and throw away the key. *(In an aggrieved tone)* Why did you do it, Wally? How could you have done such an incredible thing?

MAGRUDER *(After a moment's contemplation)* It wasn't incredible, Lineweaver. It's the only thing I could have done.

LINEWEAVER Wally, just between the two of us, you *did* give Dr. Glanz a terrible scare. He was so upset that I had to give him three grains of Nembutal. Funny, he went off to sleep in his quarters all curled up shivering as if he had a chill and sucking his thumb like a baby. I never saw anything like it. *(Pauses)* And you know another thing?

MAGRUDER What's that?

LINEWEAVER It never happened before. I mean, he spoke to me in the first person singular. He said "I"—not *"we"*— he said . . . *"I-I* gotta go to bed!" *(Shakes his head)* Fantastic! *(He exits, stage left.* MAGRUDER *sits down to write his letter. As he writes, the portable radio plays music, interrupted by a brief news broadcast announcing large victories by General MacArthur's army forces in the South Pacific. Finally he puts the letter into an envelope, seals it and looks up at* SCHWARTZ*)*

MAGRUDER How's it going, Schwartz? Feeling any better?

SCHWARTZ Yeah, Wally. The shots, they make me feel better.

MAGRUDER   That's great. I'm betting my money you're out of here in a week.

SCHWARTZ   Maybe, Wally. Maybe so. Anyway, *you're* getting out of here. That's for sure. You're a fuckin' lucky man.

MAGRUDER   Yeah, Schwartz. I guess I am lucky. I guess anyone who gets out of here is lucky. You know, even going to the brig and all—a court-martial, prison, *anything* after this—I couldn't care less, really. It'll seem like being set free! *(He draws close to* SCHWARTZ *'s bed)* And you know another thing, Schwartz? Whatever else, I think I've gotten rid of my hypochondria. Breathe on me, Schwartz! *(With a faint smile,* SCHWARTZ *exhales in his face)* Fantastic. The breath of a babe! It was like a zephyr!
   *(*LINEWEAVER *enters from stage left and approaches the* MARINE CORPORAL *with some papers; the latter gives them a brief glance, then comes toward* MAGRUDER*)*

MARINE CORPORAL   All right, marine, grab your seabag and let's get going.

LINEWEAVER   Write me a letter from Portsmouth. I'm going to miss you, sonny boy. *(As* MAGRUDER *and the* CORPORAL *exit, he goes to* SCHWARTZ *'s bedside. He looks down at him, then sits on the edge of the bed and picks up the pet shop book)* Where were you reading, Schwartz?

SCHWARTZ   *(Very weakly)*   I think it was the small dogs I was reading about. Yeah, the small dogs.

LINEWEAVER   *(Begins to read as, very slowly, the sound of "There's a Star-Spangled Banner Waving Somewhere" rises up and over his voice)* "Dollar-wise and pound for pound, the friendly, frolicsome Chihuahua is one of the most attractive items in the pet shop inventory. Another lovable

little bundle of fun from south of the border is the frisky
Mexican Hairless. Women will comprise most of your
customers for these small breeds, as they may be carried
about in handbags and are great to fondle and cuddle,
satisfying the maternal instinct. Many times I have been
asked the question by prospective pet shop owners:
Aren't these small breeds more edgy and nervous than
the larger dogs? My answer is an unqualified no. As a
veterinarian with over thirty years of experience in
handling all the canine varieties, I can testify that the
notion of smaller dogs being more neurotic is strictly a
myth . . ."

About the Author

WILLIAM STYRON was born in Newport News, Virginia. He served almost three years in the United States Marine Corps during World War II, and after the war returned to complete his studies at Duke University.

Lie Down in Darkness, William Styron's first novel, appeared in 1951. For that initial work, he was awarded the Prix de Rome of the American Academy of Arts and Letters. Two years later his short novel, *The Long March*, was published, followed by *Set This House on Fire* (1960) and *The Confessions of Nat Turner* (1967), which received the Pulitzer Prize for 1967.

76-2553

PS   Styron, William,
3569   1925-.
.T9
I5   In the clap shack

DATE			
APR 05 1984			
APR 05 1984			
APR 5 1984			
JUL 03 '91			
JUL 01 1991			
DEC 27 1991			

76-2553